# KITCHEN LIBRARY
# Starters

# KITCHEN LIBRARY
## Starters

MURDOCH BOOKS

# contents

# The Perfect Starting Point

If you are contemplating serving a starter, chances are you are planning a lunch or dinner party. Not many of us make more than one course for a regular family dinner although sometimes we might offer a simple salad or soup as a prelude to a weekday main course — and sometimes, when appetites are flagging, certain starter dishes make the perfect light meal.

With *Kitchen Library Starters* as your resource, you'll never be at a loss when planning a menu. From quiche to quail, tortellini to terrines and tarts to timbales, the starter for every occasion is now conveniently at your fingertips. This collection makes the business of choosing a starter easy for the cook. If it's a swish occasion you're hosting, look no further than the delicious seafood options, all perfect preludes to a red meat or poultry main course. In warmer weather, slices of seafood terrine, an attractive selection of marinated seafood or slivers of homemade gravlax with mustard sauce will entice with their refreshing, cool flavours. Watercress and duck salad with lychees or prosciutto, camembert and fig salad are equally excellent choices to serve before a seafood-based main dish, and their clever combinations of ingredients are worthy of any restaurant menu.

A starter sets the tone for everything that's to follow and its success will both raise expectations and awaken appetites. It needs to be satisfying, without being too filling, and its flavours should balance well with the rest of your menu. It should look attractive and appealing, be in tune with the season and, most importantly for the cook, it needs to easily coordinate with the preparation and serving of the main course. With so many things to consider, it's timely that *Kitchen Library Starters* brings together a fabulous assemblage of every first course recipe you could ever wish for or imagine.

# soups

# Red Gazpacho

✿ SERVES 4
✿ PREPARATION TIME: 40 MINUTES
✿ COOKING TIME: NIL

1 kg (2 lb 4 oz) vine-ripened tomatoes
2 slices day-old white Italian bread, crusts
    removed, broken into pieces
1 red capsicum (pepper), seeded,
    membrane removed and roughly
    chopped
2 garlic cloves, chopped
1 small green chilli, chopped (optional)
1 teaspoon sugar
2 tablespoons red wine vinegar
2 tablespoons extra virgin olive oil
8 ice cubes

GARNISH
½ Lebanese (short) cucumber, seeded and
    finely diced
½ red capsicum (pepper), seeded,
    membrane removed and finely diced
½ green capsicum (pepper), seeded,
    membrane removed and finely diced
½ red onion, finely diced
½ ripe tomato, diced

Score a cross in the base of the tomatoes. Put in a heatproof bowl and cover with boiling water. Leave for 30 seconds, then transfer to cold water. Drain and peel the skin away from the cross. Cut the tomatoes in half, scoop out the seeds and roughly chop.

Soak the bread in cold water for 5 minutes, then squeeze out any excess liquid. Put the bread in a food processor with the tomato, capsicum, garlic, chilli, sugar and vinegar, and process until combined and smooth.

With the motor running, add the oil to make a smooth creamy mixture. Season to taste. Refrigerate for at least 2 hours. Add a little extra vinegar, if desired.

To make the garnish, mix all the ingredients in a bowl. To serve, put 2 ice cubes in each bowl of soup and serve the garnish in separate bowls.

# Garlic, Pasta and Fish Soup

☘ SERVES 4–6
☘ PREPARATION TIME: 30 MINUTES
☘ COOKING TIME: 40 MINUTES

80 ml (2½ fl oz/⅓ cup) olive oil
1 leek, white part only, trimmed and sliced
20–30 garlic cloves, thinly sliced
2 potatoes, chopped
2 litres (70 fl oz/8 cups) fish stock
70 g (2½ oz/½ cup) small pasta shapes
10 baby (pattypan) squash, halved
2 zucchini (courgettes), cut into thick
    slices
300 g (10½ oz) ling fillets, chopped into
    large pieces
1–2 tablespoons lemon juice
2 tablespoons shredded basil

Heat the oil in a large saucepan, add the leek, garlic and potato and cook over medium heat for 10 minutes. Add 500 ml (17 fl oz/2 cups) of the stock and cook for 10 minutes. Allow to cool slightly before transferring to a food processor or blender and blending, in batches, until smooth.

Pour the remaining stock into the pan and bring to the boil. Add the pasta, squash and zucchini. Add the purée, and simmer for 15 minutes. When the pasta is soft, add the fish pieces and cook for 5 minutes, or until tender. Add the lemon juice and basil, and season to taste.

# French Onion Soup

☘ SERVES 4–6
☘ PREPARATION TIME: 20 MINUTES
☘ COOKING TIME: 1 HOUR 45 MINUTES

60 g (2¼ oz) butter
6 onions (about 1 kg/2 lb 4 oz), sliced into
    fine rings
1 teaspoon sugar
3 tablespoons plain (all-purpose) flour
2.25 litres (79 fl oz/9 cups) vegetable stock
1 baguette, cut into 1 cm (½ inch) slices
65 g (2½ oz/½ cup) grated gruyère or
    cheddar cheese, plus extra, to serve

Melt the butter in a large saucepan. Add the onion and cook slowly over low heat for about 20 minutes, or until tender. Add the sugar and flour and cook, stirring, for 1–2 minutes until the mixture is just starting to turn golden. Add the stock and bring to a simmer. Cover, and continue to cook over low heat for 1 hour, stirring occasionally. Season to taste.

Preheat the oven to 180°C (350°F/Gas 4). Bake the baguette slices for 20 minutes, turning once, until dry and golden. Top each slice with some of the grated cheese and place under a hot grill (broiler) until the cheese is melted. Serve the soup topped with the toasted cheese croutons. Sprinkle with extra grated cheese.

*Garlic, Pasta and Fish Soup*

# Spicy Chicken Broth with Coriander Pasta

❀ SERVES 4
❀ PREPARATION TIME: 1 HOUR
❀ COOKING TIME: 50 MINUTES

350 g (12 oz) chicken thighs or wings,
    skin removed
2 carrots, finely chopped
2 celery stalks, finely chopped
2 small leeks, white part only, finely
    chopped
3 egg whites
1.5 litres (52 fl oz/6 cups) chicken stock
Tabasco sauce

CORIANDER PASTA
60 g (2¼ oz/½ cup) plain (all-purpose)
    flour
1 egg
½ teaspoon sesame oil
90 g (3¼ oz) coriander (cilantro) leaves

Put the chicken pieces, carrot, celery and leek in a large heavy-based saucepan. Push the chicken to one side and add the egg whites to the vegetables. Using a wire whisk, beat for a minute or so, until frothy (take care not to use a pan that can be scratched by the whisk).

Warm the stock in a separate saucepan, then gradually add the stock to the first pan, whisking continuously to froth the egg whites. Continue whisking while slowly bringing to the boil. Make a hole in the froth on top with a spoon and leave to simmer for 30 minutes, without stirring.

Line a large strainer with a damp tea towel (dish towel) or double thickness of muslin (cheesecloth) and strain the broth into a clean bowl (discard the chicken and vegetables). Season with salt, pepper and Tabasco sauce to taste. Set aside until you are ready to serve.

To make the coriander pasta, sift the flour into a bowl and make a well in the centre. Whisk the egg and oil together and pour into the well. Mix together to make a soft pasta dough and knead on a lightly floured surface for 2 minutes, until smooth.

Divide the pasta dough into four even portions. Roll one portion out very thinly and cover with a layer of evenly spaced coriander leaves. Roll out another portion of pasta and lay this on top of the leaves, then gently roll the layers together. Repeat with the remaining pasta and coriander.

Cut out squares of pasta around the leaves. The pasta may then be left to sit and dry out if it is not needed immediately. When you are ready to serve, heat the chicken broth gently in a pan. As the broth simmers, add the pasta and cook for 1 minute. Serve immediately.

# Carrot and Coriander Soup

🌺 SERVES 4
🌺 PREPARATION TIME: 15 MINUTES
🌺 COOKING TIME: 1 HOUR 10 MINUTES

2 tablespoons olive oil
1 onion, chopped
800 g (1 lb 12 oz) carrots, roughly chopped
1 bay leaf
1 teaspoon ground cumin
1 teaspoon cayenne pepper
1 teaspoon ground coriander
2 teaspoons paprika
1.25 litres (44 fl oz/5 cups) chicken or
    vegetable stock
250 g (9 oz/1 cup) Greek-style yoghurt
2 tablespoons chopped coriander (cilantro)
    leaves
coriander (cilantro) leaves, extra,
    to garnish

Heat the oil in a saucepan, add the onion and carrot and cook over low heat for 30 minutes. Add the bay leaf and spices and cook for a further 2 minutes. Add the stock, bring to the boil, then reduce the heat and simmer, uncovered, for 40 minutes, or until the carrot is tender. Allow to cool slightly, before transferring to a food processor and blending, in batches, until smooth. Return to a clean saucepan and gently reheat. Season to taste.

Combine the yoghurt and chopped coriander in a bowl. Pour the soup into bowls and serve with a dollop of the yoghurt mixture. Garnish with coriander leaves.

# Cream of Oyster Soup

🌺 SERVES 4
🌺 PREPARATION TIME: 15 MINUTES
🌺 COOKING TIME: 20 MINUTES

18 fresh oysters, on the half shell
15 g (¹/₂ oz) butter
1 small onion, finely chopped
125 ml (4 fl oz/¹/₂ cup) white wine
375 ml (13 fl oz/1¹/₂ cups) fish stock
250 ml (9 fl oz/1 cup) pouring
    (whipping) cream
6 whole black peppercorns
6 basil leaves, torn
1 teaspoon lime juice
spring onions (scallions), shredded,
    to garnish
basil leaves, extra, shredded, to garnish

Drain the oysters in a small strainer and reserve the juice and oysters separately. Roughly chop six of the oysters. Melt the butter in a small saucepan and add the onion. Cover and cook over low heat until soft but not brown, stirring occasionally. Add the wine and simmer for 5 minutes, or until reduced by half.

Add the stock to the pan, simmer for 2 minutes, then add the cream, peppercorns, basil and chopped oysters and simmer for 5 minutes. Strain, then push the mixture against the sides of the strainer, to extract as much flavour as possible. Discard the solids in the strainer.

Return the liquid to the pan and bring to the boil. Add the lime juice and reserved oyster juice. Season to taste. Spoon into four small bowls and add three oysters to each. Top with cracked black pepper. Garnish with spring onion and basil.

*Carrot and Coriander Soup*

# Spicy Tomato and Pea Soup

❀ SERVES 6
❀ PREPARATION TIME: 15 MINUTES
❀ COOKING TIME: 20–25 MINUTES

6 large very ripe tomatoes, chopped
2 tablespoons ghee or butter
1 large onion, thinly sliced
1 garlic clove, crushed
2 teaspoons ground coriander
2 teaspoons ground cumin
1/2 teaspoon fennel seeds
2 bay leaves
1 green chilli, seeded and sliced
375 ml (13 fl oz/1 1/2 cups) coconut cream
235 g (8 1/2 oz/1 1/2 cups) frozen peas
1 tablespoon sugar
1 tablespoon chopped mint

In a saucepan, simmer the tomato in about 500 ml (17 fl oz/2 cups) water until very tender. Allow to cool slightly before transferring to a food processor and blending, in batches, until smooth.

Heat the ghee in a large saucepan, add the onion and garlic and cook over medium heat until very soft. Add the coriander, cumin, fennel seeds, bay leaves and chilli, and cook, stirring, for 1 minute. Add the coconut cream and the puréed tomatoes, and bring to the boil. Reduce the heat, add the peas and cook until tender. Remove the bay leaves, add the sugar and mint, and season with freshly ground pepper to taste.

# New England Clam Chowder

❋ SERVES 4

❋ PREPARATION TIME: 35 MINUTES

❋ COOKING TIME: 45 MINUTES

1.5 kg (3 lb 5 oz) clams (vongole) or pipis,
    in shell
2 teaspoons oil
3 bacon slices, chopped
1 onion, chopped
1 garlic clove, crushed
750 g (1 lb 10 oz) potatoes, cut into dice
310 ml (10¾ fl oz/1¼ cups) fish stock
500 ml (17 fl oz/2 cups) milk
125 ml (4 fl oz/½ cup) pouring
    (whipping) cream
3 tablespoons chopped flat-leaf (Italian)
    parsley

Discard any clams that are broken, already open or do not close when tapped on the bench. If necessary, soak in cold water for 1–2 hours to remove any grit. Drain and put in a large heavy-based saucepan with 250 ml (9 fl oz/1 cup) water. Cover and simmer over low heat for 5 minutes, or until open. Discard any that do not open. Strain and reserve the liquid. Remove the clam meat from the shells.

Heat the oil in a clean saucepan. Add the bacon, onion and garlic and cook, stirring, over medium heat until the onion is soft and the bacon golden. Add the potato and stir well.

Measure the reserved clam liquid and add water to make 310 ml (10¾ fl oz/1¼ cups). Add to the pan with the stock and milk. Bring to the boil, reduce the heat, cover and simmer for 20 minutes, or until the potato is tender. Uncover and simmer for 10 minutes, or until slightly thickened. Add the cream, clam meat and parsley and season to taste. Heat through gently before serving, but do not allow to boil or the liquid may curdle.

# Pappa al Pomodoro

🌿 SERVES 4

🌿 PREPARATION TIME: 25 MINUTES

🌿 COOKING TIME: 25 MINUTES

750 g (1 lb 10 oz) vine-ripened tomatoes
1 loaf (about 450 g/1 lb) day-old crusty
    Italian bread
1 tablespoon olive oil
3 garlic cloves, crushed
1 tablespoon tomato paste (concentrated
    purée)
1.25 litres (44 fl oz/5 cups) hot vegetable
    stock or water
1 tablespoon torn basil leaves
2–3 tablespoons extra virgin olive oil,
    plus extra, to serve

Score a cross in the base of the tomatoes. Put in a heatproof bowl and cover with boiling water. Leave for 30 seconds, then transfer to cold water. Drain and peel the skin away from the cross. Cut the tomatoes in half, scoop out the seeds and chop the flesh.

Discard most of the crust from the bread and tear the bread into 3 cm (1¼ inch) pieces.

Heat the olive oil in a large saucepan. Add the garlic, tomato and tomato paste, then reduce the heat and simmer, stirring occasionally, for 10–15 minutes, or until reduced. Add the stock and bring to the boil, stirring for about 3 minutes. Reduce the heat to medium, add the bread pieces and cook, stirring, for 5 minutes, or until the bread softens and absorbs most of the liquid. Add more stock or water if the soup is too thick. Remove from the heat. Stir in the basil leaves and extra virgin olive oil, and leave for 5 minutes so the flavours have time to develop. Serve drizzled with a little extra virgin olive oil.

# Pasta and Bean Soup

🌿 SERVES 4–6

🌿 PREPARATION TIME: 20 MINUTES

🌿 COOKING TIME: 1 HOUR 25 MINUTES

250 g (9 oz) borlotti (cranberry) beans,
    soaked in water overnight
1 ham hock
1 onion, chopped
pinch ground cinnamon
pinch cayenne pepper
2 teaspoons olive oil
500 ml (17 fl oz/2 cups) chicken stock
125 g (4½ oz) tagliatelle (plain or
    spinach), broken into short lengths

Drain and rinse the borlotti beans, cover with cold water in a saucepan and bring to the boil. Stir, lower the heat and simmer for 15 minutes.

Drain the beans and transfer to a large saucepan with a tight-fitting lid. Add the ham hock, onion, cinnamon, cayenne, olive oil and stock, and enough cold water to cover. Cover and simmer over low heat for 1 hour, or until the beans are cooked and have begun to thicken the stock. Remove the hock and cut off any meat. Chop the meat and return it to the pan, discarding the bone. Season to taste.

When ready to serve, bring the soup back to the boil, toss in the tagliatelle and cook until *al dente*. Remove the pan from the heat and set aside for 1–2 minutes before serving.

*Pappa al Pomodoro*

# Rissoni and Mushroom Broth

90 g (3¼ oz) butter
2 garlic cloves, sliced
2 large onions, sliced
375 g (13 oz) mushrooms, thinly sliced
1.25 litres (44 fl oz/5 cups) chicken stock
125 g (4½ oz) rissoni
310 ml (10¾ fl oz/1¼ cups) pouring
   (whipping) cream

Melt the butter in a large saucepan over low heat. Add the garlic and onion and cook for 1 minute. Add the mushrooms and cook gently, without colouring, for 5 minutes. (Set aside a few mushroom slices to use as garnish.) Add the chicken stock and cook for 10 minutes. Allow to cool slightly before transferring to a food processor and blending until smooth.

Meanwhile, add the rissoni to a large saucepan of rapidly boiling salted water and cook until *al dente*. Drain and set aside.

Return the soup to a clean pan and stir in the rissoni and cream. Heat through and season to taste. Garnish with the reserved mushrooms.

# Prawn and Basil Soup

❀ SERVES 4

❀ PREPARATION TIME: 45 MINUTES

❀ COOKING TIME: 15–20 MINUTES

500 g (1 lb 2 oz) raw prawns (shrimp)
2 tablespoons olive oil
20 g (¾ oz) butter
2 garlic cloves
1 small red onion, thinly sliced
2 celery stalks, cut into thin batons
3 small carrots, cut into thin batons
1 tablespoon finely chopped flat-leaf
   (Italian) parsley
1½ tablespoons finely chopped basil
pinch cayenne pepper
125 ml (4 fl oz/½ cup) dry sherry
1 litre (35 fl oz/4 cups) chicken stock
70 g (2½ oz) conchiglie (shell pasta)
60 ml (2 fl oz/¼ cup) pouring (whipping)
   cream

Peel the prawns and gently pull out the dark vein from each prawn back, starting from the head end.

In a large saucepan, heat the oil and butter. Add the garlic cloves and the onion and cook over low heat for 2–3 minutes. Add the celery and carrot and fry until the vegetables are golden, but not brown. Add the parsley, basil and cayenne pepper. Stir briefly, add the prawns and toss through. Remove the garlic cloves. Pour in the sherry, increase the heat and cook for 2–3 minutes. Add the chicken stock, bring back to the boil, reduce the heat and simmer for 5 minutes. Add the conchiglie and simmer until the pasta is *al dente*. Stir in the cream and season to taste.

*Rissoni and Mushroom Broth*

# Crab and Corn Eggflower Noodle Broth

- SERVES 4
- PREPARATION TIME: 15 MINUTES
- COOKING TIME: 15 MINUTES

70 g (2 1/2 oz) dried thin egg noodles
1 tablespoon peanut oil
1 teaspoon finely chopped fresh ginger
3 spring onions (scallions), thinly sliced
1.5 litres (52 fl oz/6 cups) chicken stock
80 ml (2 1/2 fl oz/1/3 cup) mirin
250 g (9 oz) fresh baby corn, sliced on the diagonal into 1 cm (1/2 inch) slices
175 g (6 oz) fresh crabmeat
1 tablespoon cornflour (cornstarch), mixed with 1 tablespoon water
2 eggs, lightly beaten
2 teaspoons lime juice
1 tablespoon soy sauce
3 tablespoons torn coriander (cilantro) leaves

Cook the noodles in a large saucepan of boiling salted water for 3 minutes, or until just tender. Drain, then rinse under cold water. Set aside.

Heat a non-stick wok over high heat, add the peanut oil and swirl to coat the side of the wok. Add the ginger and white part of the spring onion and cook over medium heat for 1–2 minutes. Add the stock, mirin and corn and bring to the boil, then simmer for 3 minutes. Stir in the noodles, crabmeat and cornflour mixture. Return to a simmer and stir constantly until it thickens. Reduce the heat and pour in the egg in a thin stream, stirring constantly — do not boil. Gently stir in the lime juice, soy sauce and half the coriander.

Divide the noodles among four bowls and ladle on the soup. Top with the green spring onion and remaining coriander leaves.

# Ajo Blanco

- SERVES 4–6
- PREPARATION TIME: 20 MINUTES
- COOKING TIME: 3 MINUTES

1 loaf (200 g/7 oz) day-old white Italian bread
150 g (5 1/2 oz/1 cup) blanched almonds
3–4 garlic cloves, chopped
125 ml (4 fl oz/1/2 cup) extra virgin olive oil
80 ml (2 1/2 fl oz/1/3 cup) sherry (or white wine vinegar)
375 ml (13 fl oz/1 1/2 cups) vegetable stock
2 tablespoons olive oil, extra
80 g (2 3/4 oz) day-old white Italian bread, extra, crust removed, cut into cubes
200 g (7 oz) small seedless green grapes

Slice and remove the crusts from the bread, soak in cold water for 5 minutes, then squeeze out any excess liquid. Chop the almonds and garlic in a processor until well ground. Add the bread and process until smooth.

With the motor running, add the extra virgin olive oil in a slow steady stream until the mixture is the consistency of thick mayonnaise. Slowly add the sherry and about 310 ml (10 3/4 fl oz/1 1/4 cups) of stock. Blend for 1 minute. Season with salt. Refrigerate for at least 2 hours. The soup thickens on refrigeration so you may need to add the remaining stock or water to thin it.

When ready to serve, heat the olive oil in a frying pan, add the bread cubes and toss over medium heat for 2–3 minutes, or until golden. Drain on paper towel. Serve the soup very cold. Garnish with bread cubes and grapes.

*Crab and Corn Eggflower Noodle Broth*

# Lobster Bisque

* SERVES 4–6
* PREPARATION TIME: 20 MINUTES
* COOKING TIME: 1 HOUR

1 raw lobster tail, about 400 g (14 oz)
90 g (3¼ oz) butter
1 large onion, chopped
1 large carrot, chopped
1 celery stalk, chopped
60 ml (2 fl oz/¼ cup) brandy
250 ml (9 fl oz/1 cup) white wine
6 parsley sprigs
1 thyme sprig
2 bay leaves
1 tablespoon tomato paste (concentrated
    purée)
1 litre (35 fl oz/4 cups) fish stock
2 tomatoes, chopped
2 tablespoons rice flour or cornflour
    (cornstarch)
125 ml (4 fl oz/½ cup) pouring
    (whipping) cream

Remove the meat from the lobster tail. Wash the shell and crush into large pieces with a mallet or rolling pin, then set aside. Chop the meat into small pieces, cover and chill.

Melt the butter in a large saucepan, add the onion, carrot and celery and cook over low heat for about 20 minutes, stirring occasionally, until the vegetables are softened but not brown.

In a small saucepan, heat the brandy, set alight with a long match and carefully pour over the vegetables. Shake the pan until the flame dies down. Add the white wine and the lightly crushed lobster shell. Increase the heat and boil until the liquid is reduced by half. Add the parsley, thyme, bay leaves, tomato paste, fish stock and chopped tomato. Simmer, uncovered, for 25 minutes, stirring occasionally. Strain the mixture through a fine sieve or dampened muslin (cheesecloth), pressing gently to extract all the liquid. Discard the vegetables and lobster shell. Return the liquid to a clean pan.

Blend the rice flour or cornflour with the cream in a small bowl. Add to the liquid and stir over medium heat until the mixture boils and thickens. Add the lobster meat and season to taste. Cook, without boiling, for 10 minutes, or until the lobster is just cooked. Serve hot.

NOTE: If you don't dampen the muslin when straining the mixture, it will soak up too much of the liquid.

# Pumpkin Soup with Harissa

🌸 SERVES 6
🌸 PREPARATION TIME: 10–40 MINUTES
🌸 COOKING TIME: 25 MINUTES

2.5 kg (5 lb 8 oz) pumpkin (winter
   squash)
750 ml (26 fl oz/3 cups) vegetable stock
750 ml (26 fl oz/3 cups) milk
sugar, to taste

HARISSA
250 g (9 oz) fresh or dried red chillies
1 tablespoon caraway seeds
1 tablespoon coriander seeds
2 teaspoons cumin seeds
4–6 garlic cloves
1 tablespoon dried mint
125 ml (4 fl oz/$\frac{1}{2}$ cup) extra virgin
   olive oil

Remove the skin, seeds and fibre from the pumpkin and cut into pieces. Simmer, uncovered, in a large saucepan with the stock and milk for 15–20 minutes or until tender. Allow to cool slightly before transferring to a food processor, and blending, in batches, until smooth. Season with a little sugar and black pepper. Return to a clean saucepan and gently reheat until ready to serve.

To make the harissa, wearing rubber gloves, remove the stems of the chillies, split in half, remove the seeds and soften the flesh in hot water for 5 minutes (or 30 minutes if using dried). Drain and place in a food processor.

While the chillies are soaking, dry-fry the caraway, coriander and cumin seeds in a frying pan for about 1–2 minutes, or until aromatic. Add the spices, garlic, mint and 1 teaspoon salt to the food processor and, slowly adding the olive oil, process until a smooth, thick paste forms. Stir the harissa into bowls of soup.

# Melokhia Soup

🌸 SERVES 4
🌸 PREPARATION TIME: 20 MINUTES
🌸 COOKING TIME: 35 MINUTES

1.25 litres (44 fl oz/5 cups) chicken stock
1 onion, halved
6 cracked cardamom pods
2 silverbeet (Swiss chard) leaves, chopped
400 g (14 oz) frozen shredded melokhia
   leaves
2 tablespoons ghee
4 garlic cloves, crushed
1 teaspoon ground coriander
pinch chilli powder

DRESSING
1 small onion, finely chopped
2 tablespoons lemon juice

Put the stock, onion and cardamom pods in a large saucepan, bring to the boil and boil for 12–15 minutes, or until the stock reduces to about 1 litre (35 fl oz/ 4 cups). Remove the onion and cardamom with a slotted spoon. Add the silverbeet and melokhia leaves to the pan. Bring to the boil, reduce the heat and simmer, uncovered, for 10 minutes.

Meanwhile, heat the ghee in a small saucepan and add the garlic and $\frac{1}{4}$ teaspoon salt. Cook over low heat, stirring constantly, until the garlic is golden. Remove from the heat and stir in the coriander and chilli.

To make the dressing, combine the ingredients in a small serving bowl. Set aside.

Stir the garlic mixture into the soup and simmer for 2 minutes. Serve with the dressing on the side.

*Pumpkin Soup with Harissa*

# Tom Kha Gai

❀ SERVES 4
❀ PREPARATION TIME: 20 MINUTES
❀ COOKING TIME: 20 MINUTES

5 cm (2 inch) piece fresh galangal, thinly
    sliced
500 ml (17 fl oz/2 cups) coconut milk
250 ml (9 fl oz/1 cup) chicken stock
600 g (1 lb 5 oz) boneless, skinless
    chicken breasts, cut into thin strips
1–2 teaspoons finely chopped red chilli
2 tablespoons fish sauce
1 teaspoon soft brown sugar
10 g (¼ oz) coriander (cilantro) leaves
coriander (cilantro) sprigs, to garnish

Combine the galangal, coconut milk and chicken stock in a saucepan. Bring to the boil, then reduce the heat and simmer over low heat for 10 minutes, stirring occasionally. Add the chicken and chilli to the pan and simmer for 8 minutes. Add the fish sauce and sugar and stir to combine. Add the coriander leaves and serve immediately, garnished with coriander sprigs.

# Yoghurt Soup

❀ SERVES 4–6
❀ PREPARATION TIME: 15 MINUTES
❀ COOKING TIME: 20 MINUTES

1.5 litres (52 fl oz/6 cups) vegetable stock
70 g (2½ oz/⅓ cup) short-grain white
    rice
80 g (2¾ oz) butter
50 g (1¾ oz) plain (all-purpose) flour
250 g (9 oz/1 cup) plain yoghurt
1 egg yolk
1 tablespoon finely sliced mint leaves
¼ teaspoon cayenne pepper

Put the stock and rice in a saucepan and bring to the boil over high heat. Reduce the heat to medium–low and simmer for 10 minutes, then remove from heat and set aside.

In another saucepan, melt 60 g (2¼ oz) of the butter over low heat. Stir in the flour and cook for 2–3 minutes, or until pale and foaming. Gradually add the stock and rice mixture, stirring constantly, and cook over medium heat for 2 minutes, or until the mixture thickens slightly. Reduce the heat to low.

In a small bowl, whisk together the yoghurt and egg yolk, then gradually pour into the soup, stirring constantly. Remove from the heat and stir in the mint and ½ teaspoon salt.

Just before serving, melt the remaining butter in a small saucepan over medium heat. Add the cayenne pepper and cook until the mixture is lightly browned. Pour over the soup.

*Tom Kha Gai*

# Bourride

- SERVES 8
- PREPARATION TIME: 25 MINUTES
- COOKING TIME: 1 HOUR 10 MINUTES

CROUTONS
1 tablespoon butter
1 tablespoon olive oil
4 slices white bread, crusts removed and cut into 1.5 cm (5/8 inch) cubes

2 kg (4 lb 8 oz) assorted firm white fish fillets (such as bass, whiting and cod)
5 egg yolks
4 garlic cloves, crushed
3–5 teaspoons lemon juice
250 ml (9 fl oz/1 cup) olive oil

STOCK
80 ml (2 1/2 fl oz/1/3 cup) olive oil
1 large onion, chopped
1 carrot, sliced
1 leek, white part only, chopped
420 ml (14 1/2 fl oz/1 2/3 cups) dry white wine
1 teaspoon dried fennel seeds
2 garlic cloves, bruised
2 bay leaves
1 large strip orange zest
2 thyme sprigs

To make the croutons, heat the butter and oil in a heavy-based frying pan. When the butter begins to foam, add the bread cubes and cook for 5 minutes, or until golden. Drain on crumpled paper towel. Set aside.

Fillet the fish (or ask your fishmonger to do it), reserving the heads and bones for the stock.

To make the aïoli, put 2 of the egg yolks, garlic and 3 teaspoons lemon juice in a food processor and blend until creamy. With the motor still running, slowly drizzle in the oil. Season and add the remaining lemon juice, to taste. Set aside until needed.

To make the stock, heat the olive oil in large saucepan or stockpot and add the onion, carrot and leek. Cook over low heat for 12–15 minutes, or until the vegetables are soft. Add the fish heads and bones, wine, fennel seeds, garlic, bay leaves, orange zest, thyme, black pepper and 1/2 teaspoon salt. Cover with 2 litres (70 fl oz/8 cups) water. Bring to the boil and skim off the froth. Reduce the heat and simmer for 30 minutes. Strain into a pot, crushing the bones well to release as much flavour as possible. Return to the heat.

Preheat the oven to 120°C (235°F/Gas 1/2). Cut the fish fillets into large pieces about 9 cm (3 1/2 inches) long. Add to the stock and bring to a simmer, putting the heavier pieces in first and adding the more delicate pieces later. Poach for 6–8 minutes, until the flesh starts to become translucent. Transfer the fish pieces to a platter and moisten with a little stock. Cover with foil and keep warm.

Place 8 tablespoons of the aïoli in a large bowl and slowly add the remaining 3 egg yolks, stirring constantly. Ladle a little stock into the aïoli mixture, blend well and return slowly to the rest of the stock. Stir with a wooden spoon for 8–10 minutes over low heat, or until the soup has thickened and coats the back of a spoon. Do not boil or the mixture will curdle.

To serve, scatter the fish pieces into bowls and ladle the stock over over the top. Sprinkle with croutons.

# Pie-Crust Mushroom Soup

🌷 PREPARATION TIME: 25 MINUTES

🌷 COOKING TIME: 35 MINUTES

400 g (14 oz) large field mushrooms
60 g (2¼ oz) butter
1 onion, finely chopped
1 garlic clove, crushed
30 g (1 oz/¼ cup) plain (all-purpose) flour
750 ml (26 fl oz/3 cups) chicken stock
2 tablespoons thyme leaves
2 tablespoons sherry
250 ml (9 fl oz/1 cup) pouring (whipping) cream
1 sheet frozen puff pastry, thawed
1 egg, lightly beaten

Preheat the oven to 200°C (400°F/Gas 6). Peel and roughly chop the mushrooms, including the stems.

Melt the butter in a large saucepan, add the onion and cook over medium heat for 3 minutes, or until soft. Add the garlic and cook for 1 minute. Add the mushrooms and cook until soft. Sprinkle with the flour and stir for 1 minute. Stir in the stock and thyme and bring to the boil. Reduce the heat and simmer, covered, for 10 minutes. Allow to cool slightly before transferring to a food processor and blending, in batches.

Return the soup to the pan, stir in the sherry and cream then pour into four ovenproof bowls (use small, deep bowls rather than wide shallow ones, or the pastry may sag into the soup).

Cut rounds of pastry slightly larger than the bowl tops and cover each bowl with pastry. Seal the pastry edges and brush lightly with the egg. Place the bowls on a baking tray and bake for 15 minutes, or until golden and puffed.

# Green Pea Soup

🌺 SERVES 4–6
🌺 PREPARATION TIME: 20 MINUTES
🌺 COOKING TIME: 1 HOUR 40 MINUTES

335 g (11¾ oz/1½ cups) dried green
   split peas
2 tablespoons oil
1 onion, finely chopped
1 celery stalk, finely sliced
1 carrot, finely sliced
1 tablespoon ground cumin
1 tablespoon ground coriander
2 teaspoons grated fresh ginger
1.25 litres (44 fl oz/5 cups) vegetable
   stock
310 g (11 oz/2 cups) frozen green peas
1 tablespoon chopped mint
yoghurt or sour cream, to serve

Soak the split peas in cold water for 2 hours. Drain the peas well.

Heat the oil in a large heavy-based saucepan and add the onion, celery and carrot. Cook over medium heat for 3 minutes, stirring occasionally, until soft but not browned. Stir in the cumin, coriander and ginger, then cook for 1 minute. Add the split peas and stock to the pan. Bring to the boil, then reduce the heat to low. Simmer, covered, for 1½ hours, stirring occasionally. Add the frozen peas to the pan and stir to combine.

Allow to cool slightly before transferring to a food processor and blending, in batches, until smooth. Return to a clean pan and gently reheat. Season to taste and then stir in the mint. Serve in bowls with a swirl of yoghurt or sour cream.

# Corn Chowder

🌺 SERVES 8
🌺 PREPARATION TIME: 15 MINUTES
🌺 COOKING TIME: 30 MINUTES

90 g (3¼ oz) butter
2 large onions, finely chopped
1 garlic clove, crushed
2 teaspoons cumin seeds
1 litre (35 fl oz/4 cups) vegetable stock
2 potatoes, chopped
250 g (9 oz/1 cup) tinned creamed corn
400 g (14 oz/2 cups) corn kernels
3 tablespoons chopped flat-leaf
   (Italian) parsley
125 g (4½ oz/1 cup) grated cheddar
   cheese
2 tablespoons snipped chives, to garnish

Heat the butter in a large heavy-based saucepan. Add the onion and cook over medium–high heat for 5 minutes, or until golden. Add the garlic and cumin seeds, cook for 1 minute, stirring constantly. Add the vegetable stock and bring to the boil. Add the potatoes and reduce the heat. Simmer, uncovered, for 10 minutes.

Add the creamed corn, corn kernels and parsley. Bring to the boil, then reduce the heat and simmer for about 10 minutes. Stir through the cheese and season to taste. Heat gently until the cheese melts.

Serve immediately, sprinkled with the chives.

*Green Pea Soup*

# Zuppa di Cozze

※ SERVES 6
※ PREPARATION TIME: 25 MINUTES
※ COOKING TIME: 35 MINUTES

200 g (7 oz) ripe tomatoes
1 kg (2 lb 4 oz) black mussels
2 tablespoons olive oil
40 g (1½ oz) butter
1 leek, finely chopped
3 garlic cloves, crushed
pinch saffron threads
1 tablespoon finely chopped flat-leaf
   (Italian) parsley
1 small red chilli, finely chopped
170 ml (5½ fl oz/⅔ cup) dry white wine

Score a cross in the base of each tomato. Place in a heatproof bowl and cover with boiling water. Leave for 30 seconds, transfer to cold water, drain and peel away the skin from the cross. Cut the tomatoes in half, scoop out the seeds and finely chop the flesh.

Scrub the mussels with a stiff brush and pull out the hairy beards. Discard any broken mussels, or open ones that don't close when tapped on the bench. Rinse well.

Heat the oil and butter in a large saucepan and cook the leek and garlic over low heat until the leek is soft but not brown. Add the saffron, parsley and chilli and cook, stirring, for 1–2 minutes. Increase the heat and add the wine. Bring to the boil and cook for about 1–2 minutes, then add the chopped tomato and 250 ml (9 fl oz/1 cup) water. Cover and simmer for about 20 minutes.

Add the mussels to the pan and cook, covered, until they are opened. After 4–5 minutes, discard any unopened mussels. So the soup is not too crowded with shells, remove one third of the remaining mussels, remove the mussel meat and add to the soup. Discard the empty shells. Season to taste. Serve immediately with crusty bread.

# Red Capsicum Soup

❀ SERVES 6
❀ PREPARATION TIME: 20 MINUTES
❀ COOKING TIME: 30 MINUTES

4 red capsicums (peppers)
4 tomatoes
60 ml (2 fl oz/¼ cup) olive oil
½ teaspoon dried marjoram
½ teaspoon dried mixed herbs
2 garlic cloves, crushed
1 teaspoon mild curry paste
1 red onion, sliced
1 leek, white part only, sliced
250 g (9 oz) green cabbage, chopped
1 teaspoon sweet chilli sauce

Cut the capsicums into quarters. Remove the seeds and membrane. Grill (broil) until the skin blackens and blisters. Place on a cutting board, cover with a tea towel (dish towel) and allow to cool before peeling and chopping.

Score a cross in the base of the tomatoes. Put in a heatproof bowl and cover with boiling water. Leave for 30 seconds, then transfer to cold water. Drain and peel the skin away from the cross. Cut the tomatoes in half, scoop out the seeds and chop the flesh.

Heat the oil in a large saucepan. Add the herbs, garlic and curry paste. Stir over low heat for 1 minute, or until aromatic. Add the onion and leek and cook for 3 minutes or until golden. Add the cabbage, capsicum, tomato and 1 litre (35 fl oz/4 cups) water. Bring to the boil, reduce heat and simmer for 20 minutes. Remove from the heat.

Allow to cool slightly before transferring to a food processor and blending, in batches, for 30 seconds, or until smooth. Return the soup to a clean saucepan, stir through the chilli sauce and season to taste with salt and freshly ground black pepper. Reheat gently and serve hot.

# Wild Rice Soup

❋ SERVES 6
❋ PREPARATION TIME: 15 MINUTES
❋ COOKING TIME: 1 HOUR

95 g (3¼ oz/½ cup) wild rice
1 tablespoon olive oil
1 onion, finely chopped
2 celery stalks, finely chopped
1 green capsicum (pepper), seeded,
    membrane removed and finely chopped
4 back bacon slices, finely chopped
4 open cap mushrooms, thinly sliced
1 litre (35 fl oz/4 cups) chicken stock
125 ml (4 fl oz/½ cup) pouring
    (whipping) cream
1 tablespoon finely chopped flat-leaf
    (Italian) parsley

Put the wild rice in a saucepan with 500 ml (17 fl oz/ 2 cups) water and bring to the boil. Cook for 40 minutes, or until the rice is tender. Drain and rinse well.

Heat the oil in a large saucepan and add the onion, celery, capsicum and bacon. Fry for 8 minutes, or until the onion has softened and the bacon has browned. Add the mushrooms and cook for 1–2 minutes. Pour in the chicken stock and bring to the boil, then add the rice, stir, and cook the mixture for 2 minutes. Remove from the heat.

Stir in the cream and parsley, then reheat until the soup is almost boiling. Serve in deep bowls.

# Watercress Soup

❋ SERVES 4–6
❋ PREPARATION TIME: 15 MINUTES
❋ COOKING TIME: 15–20 MINUTES

100 g (3½ oz) butter
1 onion, roughly chopped
4 spring onions (scallions), roughly
    chopped
450 g (1 lb) watercress, trimmed and
    roughly chopped
40 g (1½ oz/⅓ cup) plain (all-purpose)
    flour
750 ml (26 fl oz/3 cups) vegetable stock
sour cream or pouring (whipping) cream,
    to serve

Melt the butter in a large saucepan and add the onion, spring onion and watercress. Stir over low heat for 3 minutes, or until the vegetables have softened. Add the flour and stir until combined. Gradually add the stock and 310 ml (10¾ fl oz/1¼ cups) water. Stir until smooth and the mixture boils and thickens. Simmer, covered, over low heat for 10 minutes, or until the watercress is tender.

Allow to cool slightly and transfer the mixture to a food processor and process, in batches, until smooth. Before serving, gently heat through and season to taste. Serve with a dollop of sour cream or cream.

*Wild Rice Soup*

# Avgolemono Soup with Chicken

❀ SERVES 4
❀ PREPARATION TIME: 20 MINUTES
❀ COOKING TIME: 30 MINUTES

1 onion, halved
2 whole cloves
1 carrot, cut into chunks
1 bay leaf
500 g (1 lb 2 oz) boneless, skinless
   chicken breast
70 g (2½ oz/⅓ cup) short-grain rice
3 eggs, separated
60 ml (2 fl oz/¼ cup) lemon juice
2 tablespoons chopped flat-leaf (Italian)
   parsley
4 thin lemon slices, to garnish

Stud the onion with the cloves and place in a large saucepan with 1.5 litres (52 fl oz/6 cups) water. Add the carrot, bay leaf and chicken and season. Slowly bring to the boil, then reduce the heat and simmer for 10 minutes, or until the chicken is cooked.

Strain the stock into a clean saucepan, reserving the chicken and discarding the vegetables. Add the rice to the stock, bring to the boil, then reduce the heat and simmer for 15 minutes, or until the rice is tender. Meanwhile, tear the chicken into shreds.

Whisk the egg whites in a clean dry bowl until stiff peaks form, then beat in the yolks. Slowly beat in the lemon juice. Gently stir in about 170 ml (5½ fl oz/⅔ cup) of the hot (not boiling) stock and beat thoroughly. Add the egg mixture to the stock and heat gently, but do not let it boil, otherwise the eggs may scramble. Add the chicken and season to taste.

Set aside for 2–3 minutes to allow the flavours to develop. To serve spoon into bowls, sprinkle with parsley and garnish with lemon slices.

# Scallops with Soba Noodles and Dashi Broth

❀ SERVES 4
❀ PREPARATION TIME: 10 MINUTES
❀ COOKING TIME: 15 MINUTES

250 g (9 oz) dried soba noodles
60 ml (2 fl oz/¼ cup) mirin
60 ml (2 fl oz/¼ cup) light soy sauce
2 teaspoons rice vinegar
1 teaspoon dashi granules
2 spring onions (scallions), sliced
1 teaspoon finely chopped fresh ginger
24 large scallops (without roe)
5 fresh black fungus, chopped (see Note)
1 sheet nori, shredded

Add the noodles to a large saucepan of boiling water and stir to separate. Return to the boil, adding 250 ml (9 fl oz/1 cup) cold water and repeat this step three times, as it comes to the boil. Drain and rinse under cold water.

Put the mirin, soy sauce, vinegar, dashi and 875 ml (30 fl oz/3½ cups) water in a non-stick wok. Bring to the boil, then reduce the heat and simmer for 3–4 minutes. Add the spring onion and ginger and keep at a gentle simmer.

Heat a chargrill pan or plate until very hot and sear the scallops in batches for 30 seconds each side. Remove from the pan. Divide the noodles and black fungus among four deep serving bowls. Pour 185 ml (6 fl oz/¾ cup) of the broth into each bowl and top with six scallops each. Garnish with the shredded nori and serve immediately.

# Prawn Bisque

❀ SERVES 4–6
❀ PREPARATION TIME: 25 MINUTES
❀ COOKING TIME: 15–20 MINUTES

500 g (1 lb 2 oz) raw prawns (shrimp)
60 g (2¼ oz) butter
2 tablespoons plain (all-purpose) flour
2 litres (70 fl oz/8 cups) fish stock
1/2 teaspoon paprika
250 ml (9 fl oz/1 cup) pouring
   (whipping) cream
80 ml (2½ fl oz/⅓ cup) dry sherry
1–2 tablespoons pouring (whipping)
   cream, extra, to serve
paprika, extra, to garnish

Peel the prawns and gently pull out the dark vein from each prawn back, starting at the head end. Reserve the heads and shells.

Heat the butter in a saucepan, add the prawn heads and shells and cook, stirring, over medium heat for 5 minutes, lightly crushing the heads with a wooden spoon. Add the flour and stir until combined. Add the fish stock and paprika and stir until the mixture boils. Reduce the heat and simmer, covered, over low heat, for 10 minutes. Strain the mixture through a fine sieve, then return the liquid to the pan. Add the prawns and cook over low heat for 2–3 minutes. Allow to cool slightly, then transfer to a food processor and blend, in batches, until smooth. Return the mixture to the pan. Add the cream and sherry to the pan and stir to heat through. Season to taste. Serve topped with a swirl of cream and sprinkled with paprika.

*Scallops With Soba Noodles And Dashi Broth*

# Creamy Corn and Tomato Soup

❀ SERVES 4–6
❀ PREPARATION TIME: 20 MINUTES
❀ COOKING TIME: 15 MINUTES

1 teaspoon olive oil
1 teaspoon vegetable stock (bouillon)
    powder
1 onion, finely chopped
3 tomatoes
425 g (15 oz) tomato paste (concentrated
    purée)
310 g (11 oz) tinned creamed corn
125 g (4½ oz) tinned corn kernels,
    drained
chilli powder, to taste
sour cream and tortillas, to serve

Heat the oil in a large saucepan. Add the stock powder and onion and cook until the onion is soft.

Score a cross in the base of the tomatoes. Put in a heatproof bowl and cover with boiling water. Leave for 30 seconds, then transfer to cold water. Drain and peel the skin away from the cross. Cut each tomato in half, scoop out the seeds and chop the flesh.

Add the tomato to the pan with the tomato paste, creamed corn and corn kernels. Season with chilli. Stir until heated through. Serve with a dollop of sour cream and some warm tortillas.

# Turkey and Corn Soup

❀ SERVES 4
❀ PREPARATION TIME: 10 MINUTES
❀ COOKING TIME: 20 MINUTES

20 g (¾ oz) butter
1 leek, white part only, thinly sliced
875 ml (30 fl oz/3½ cups) chicken stock
425 g (15 oz) tinned creamed corn
250 g (9 oz) shredded cooked turkey

Melt the butter in a large saucepan, add the leek and stir over medium heat for 5 minutes, or until soft. Add the chicken stock and creamed corn and stir through. Season to taste. Bring to the boil, then reduce the heat and simmer, covered, for 5 minutes. Add the turkey to the pan and stir until heated through. Serve immediately.

*Creamy Corn And Tomato Soup*

# Lemon-Scented Broth with Tortellini

🌼 SERVES 4–6

🌼 PREPARATION TIME: 10 MINUTES

🌼 COOKING TIME: 20 MINUTES

1 lemon

125 ml (4 fl oz/½ cup) white wine

440 g (15½ oz) tinned chicken consommé

375 g (13 oz) fresh or dried veal or
    chicken tortellini

4 tablespoons chopped flat-leaf (Italian)
    parsley

Using a vegetable peeler, peel wide strips from the lemon. Remove the white pith with a small sharp knife. Cut three of the wide pieces into fine strips and set aside for garnishing.

Combine the remaining wide lemon strips, white wine, consommé and 750 ml (26 fl oz/3 cups) water in a large saucepan. Cook for 10 minutes over low heat. Remove the lemon zest from the pan and bring the mixture to the boil. Add the tortellini and parsley and season with black pepper. Cook for 6–7 minutes, or until the pasta is *al dente*. Garnish with fine strips of lemon zest.

# Garlic Soup

🌼 SERVES 4

🌼 PREPARATION TIME: 15 MINUTES

🌼 COOKING TIME: 45 MINUTES

1 garlic bulb

2 large thyme sprigs

1 litre (35 fl oz/4 cups) chicken stock

80 ml (2½ fl oz/⅓ cup) pouring
    (whipping) cream

4 thick slices white bread, crusts removed

thyme leaves, to garnish

Preheat the oven to 180°C (350°F/Gas 4). Crush the cloves (about 20) from the garlic bulb, using the side of a knife. Discard the skin and put the garlic in a large saucepan with the thyme sprigs, chicken stock and 250 ml (9 fl oz/1 cup) water. Bring to the boil, then reduce the heat and simmer, uncovered, for 20 minutes. Strain through a fine sieve into a clean saucepan. Add the cream and reheat gently without allowing to boil. Season to taste.

Meanwhile, cut the bread into bite-sized cubes. Spread on a baking tray and bake for 5–10 minutes, or until lightly golden. Distribute among four soup bowls, then pour the soup over the bread. Garnish with thyme leaves and serve immediately.

*Lemon-Scented Broth with Tortellini*

# Soupe Au Pistou

🌽 SERVES 8

🌽 PREPARATION TIME: 45 MINUTES

🌽 COOKING TIME: 35 MINUTES

2 ripe tomatoes
3 flat-leaf (Italian) parsley stalks
1 large rosemary sprig
1 large thyme sprig
1 large marjoram sprig
60 ml (2 fl oz/¼ cup) olive oil
2 onions, thinly sliced
1 leek, white part only, thinly sliced
1 bay leaf
375 g (13 oz) pumpkin (winter squash),
    cut into small pieces
250 g (9 oz) potato, cut into small pieces
1 carrot, halved lengthways and thinly
    sliced
2 litres (70 fl oz/8 cups) vegetable stock
    or water
90 g (3¼ oz) fresh or frozen broad (fava)
    beans
80 g (2¾ oz/½ cup) fresh or frozen peas
2 small zucchini (courgettes), finely
    chopped
80 g (2¾ oz/½ cup) short macaroni or
    shell pasta

PISTOU
25 g (1 oz) basil leaves
2 large garlic cloves, crushed
80 ml (2½ fl oz/⅓ cup) olive oil
35 g (1¼ oz/⅓ cup) freshly grated
    parmesan cheese

Score a cross in the base of each tomato. Put in a heatproof bowl and cover with boiling water. Leave for 30 seconds then transfer to cold water, drain, peel away the skin from the cross and chop the flesh. Tie the parsley, rosemary, thyme and marjoram together with string.

Heat the oil in a heavy-based saucepan and add the onion and leek. Cook over low heat for 10 minutes, or until soft. Add the herb bunch, bay leaf, pumpkin, potato, carrot, 1 teaspoon salt and the stock. Cover and simmer for 10 minutes, or until vegetables are almost tender.

Add the broad beans, peas, zucchini, tomato and pasta. Cover and cook for 15 minutes, or until the vegetables are very tender and the pasta is *al dente*. Add more water if necessary. Remove the herbs, including the bay leaf.

To make the pistou, finely chop the basil and garlic in a food processor. Pour in the oil gradually, processing until smooth. Stir in the parmesan and ½ teaspoon freshly ground black pepper and serve spooned over the soup.

NOTE: The flavour of this soup improves if refrigerated overnight then gently reheated.

# Pumpkin, Prawn and Coconut Soup

❀ SERVES 4–6

❀ PREPARATION TIME: 15 MINUTES

❀ COOKING TIME: 20 MINUTES

500 g (1 lb 2 oz) pumpkin (winter
   squash), diced
80 ml (2½ fl oz/⅓ cup) lime juice
1 kg (2 lb 4 oz) raw large prawns (shrimp)
2 onions, chopped
1 small fresh red chilli, finely chopped
1 lemon grass stem, white part only,
   chopped
1 teaspoon shrimp paste
1 teaspoon sugar
375 ml (13 fl oz/1½ cups) coconut milk
1 teaspoon tamarind purée
125 ml (4 fl oz/½ cup) coconut cream
1 tablespoon fish sauce
2 tablespoons Thai basil leaves, plus extra,
   to serve

Combine the pumpkin with half the lime juice in a bowl. Peel the prawns and gently pull out the dark vein from each prawn back, starting at the head end.

Process the onion, chilli, lemon grass, shrimp paste, sugar and 60 ml (2 fl oz/¼ cup) coconut milk in a food processor until a paste forms.

Combine the paste with the remaining coconut milk, tamarind purée and 250 ml (9 fl oz/1 cup) water in a large saucepan and stir until smooth. Add the pumpkin and lime juice to the pan and bring to the boil. Reduce the heat and simmer, covered, for 10 minutes, or until the pumpkin is just tender.

Add the prawns and coconut cream, then simmer for 3 minutes, or until the prawns are just pink and cooked through. Stir in the fish sauce, the remaining lime juice and the Thai basil leaves.

To serve, pour the soup into warmed bowls and garnish with basil leaves.

# Tofu Miso Soup

※ SERVES 4
※ PREPARATION TIME: 10 MINUTES
※ COOKING TIME: 15 MINUTES

80 g (2¾ oz/½ cup) dashi granules
100 g (3½ oz) miso paste
1 tablespoon mirin
250 g (9 oz) firm tofu, cubed
1 spring onion (scallion), sliced, to serve

Using a wooden spoon, combine 1 litre (35 fl oz/ 4 cups) water and the dashi granules in a small saucepan and bring to the boil.

Combine the miso paste and mirin in a small bowl, then add to the pan. Stir the miso over medium heat, taking care not to let the mixture boil once the miso has dissolved, or it will lose flavour. Add the tofu cubes to the hot stock and heat, without boiling, over medium heat for 5 minutes. Serve in individual bowls, garnished with the spring onion.

# Chinese Chicken and Corn Soup

※ SERVES 4
※ PREPARATION TIME: 10 MINUTES
※ COOKING TIME: 15 MINUTES

750 ml (26 fl oz/3 cups) chicken stock
2 x 200 g (7 oz) boneless, skinless
    chicken breasts
3–4 corn cobs
1 tablespoon vegetable oil
4 spring onions (scallions), thinly sliced,
    white and green parts separated
1 garlic clove, crushed
2 teaspoons grated fresh ginger
310 g (11 oz) tinned creamed corn
2 tablespoons light soy sauce
1 tablespoon Chinese rice wine
1 tablespoon cornflour (cornstarch)
2 teaspoons sesame oil

Bring the stock to simmering point in a small saucepan. Add the chicken and remove the pan from the heat. Cover the pan and leave the chicken to cool in the liquid. Remove the chicken with a slotted spoon, then finely shred the meat using your fingers. Cut the corn kernels from the cobs — you should get about 400 g (14 oz/2 cups) of kernels.

Heat a wok over medium–high heat, add the oil and swirl to coat the side of the wok. Add the white part of the spring onion, the garlic and ginger and stir-fry for 30 seconds. Add the stock, corn kernels, creamed corn, soy sauce, rice wine and 250 ml (9 fl oz/1 cup) water. Stir until the soup comes to the boil, then reduce the heat and simmer for 10 minutes. Add the chicken meat.

Meanwhile, stir the cornflour, sesame oil and 1 tablespoon water together in a small bowl until smooth. Add a little of the hot stock, stir together, then pour this mixture into the soup. Bring to simmering point, stirring constantly for 3–4 minutes, or until slightly thickened. Season to taste. Garnish with the spring onion greens.

*Tofu Miso Soup*

# Creamy Red Lentil Soup

🔆 SERVES 6
🔆 PREPARATION TIME: 25 MINUTES
🔆 COOKING TIME: 1 HOUR

CROUTONS
4 thick bread slices, crusts removed
60 g (2¼ oz) butter
1 tablespoon oil

1½ teaspoons cumin seeds
80 g (2¾ oz) butter
1 large brown onion, diced
185 g (6½ oz/¾ cup) red lentils, rinsed
    and drained
1.5 litres (52 fl oz/6 cups) vegetable stock
2 tablespoons plain (all-purpose) flour
2 egg yolks
185 ml (6 fl oz/¾ cup) milk

To make the croutons, cut the bread into 1 cm (½ inch) cubes. Heat the butter and oil in a frying pan and when the butter foams, add the bread and cook over medium heat until golden and crisp. Drain on crumpled paper towel.

In a small frying pan, dry roast the cumin seeds until they start to pop and become aromatic. Leave to cool, then grind to a fine powder using a mortar and pestle.

Melt half the butter in a heavy-based saucepan and cook the onion over medium heat for 5–6 minutes, until softened. Add the lentils, ground cumin and stock and bring to the boil. Cover and simmer for 30–35 minutes, or until the lentils are very soft. Allow to cool slightly before transferring to a food processor and blending, in batches, until smooth.

In a large heavy-based saucepan, melt the remaining butter over low heat. Stir in the flour and cook for 2–3 minutes, or until pale and foaming. Stirring constantly, add the lentil purée gradually, then simmer for 4–5 minutes.

In a small bowl, combine the egg yolks and milk. Whisk a small amount of the soup into the egg mixture and then return it all to the soup, stirring constantly. Be careful not to boil the soup or the egg will curdle. Season to taste. Heat the soup to just under boiling and serve with the croutons.

# Spinach and Lentil Soup

🌸 SERVES 4–6

🌸 PREPARATION TIME: 10 MINUTES

🌸 COOKING TIME: 1 HOUR 25 MINUTES

375 g (13 oz/2 cups) brown lentils
2 teaspoons olive oil
1 onion, finely chopped
2 garlic cloves, crushed
20 English spinach leaves, stalks removed,
　　leaves finely shredded
1 teaspoon ground cumin
1 teaspoon finely grated lemon zest
500 ml (17 fl oz/2 cups) vegetable stock
2 tablespoons finely chopped coriander
　　(cilantro)

Put the lentils in a large saucepan with 1.25 litres (44 fl oz/5 cups) water. Bring to the boil and then simmer, uncovered, for 1 hour. Rinse and drain, then set aside.

In a separate saucepan heat the oil. Add the onion and garlic. Cook over medium heat until golden. Add the spinach and cook for a further 2 minutes.

Add the lentils, cumin, lemon zest, vegetable stock and 500 ml (17 fl oz/2 cups) water to the pan. Simmer, uncovered, for 15 minutes. Add the coriander and stir through. Serve immediately.

# Won Ton Soup

🌸 SERVES 4–6

🌸 PREPARATION TIME: 40 MINUTES

🌸 COOKING TIME: 5 MINUTES

4 dried Chinese mushrooms
250 g (9 oz) raw prawns (shrimp)
250 g (9 oz) minced (ground) pork
1 tablespoon soy sauce
1 teaspoon sesame oil
2 spring onions (scallions), finely chopped
1 teaspoon grated fresh ginger
2 tablespoons tinned chopped water
　　chestnuts
250 g (9 oz) packet won ton wrappers
cornflour (cornstarch), to dust
1.5 litres (52 fl oz/6 cups) chicken or beef
　　stock
4 spring onions (scallions), extra, finely
　　sliced, to garnish

Soak the mushrooms in a bowl of hot water for 30 minutes. Drain, then squeeze to remove any excess liquid. Discard the stems and chop the caps finely. Peel the prawns, gently pulling out their dark veins. Finely chop the prawn meat and mix in a bowl with the mushrooms, pork, soy sauce, sesame oil, spring onion, ginger and water chestnuts.

Cover the won ton wrappers with a damp tea towel to prevent them drying out. Working with one wrapper at a time, place a heaped teaspoon of mixture in the centre of each. Moisten the pastry edges with water, fold in half diagonally and bring the two points together. Place on a tray dusted with cornflour until ready to cook.

Cook the won tons in a saucepan of rapidly boiling water for 4–5 minutes.

In a separate saucepan bring the stock to the boil. Remove the won tons with a slotted spoon and place in serving bowls. Scatter the spring onion over the top. Ladle the stock over the won tons.

*Spinach and Lentil Soup*

# salads and vegetables

# Tomato and Bocconcini Salad

🌺 SERVES 4

🌺 PREPARATION TIME: 10 MINUTES

🌺 COOKING TIME: NIL

3 large vine-ripened tomatoes
250 g (9 oz) bocconcini (fresh baby mozzarella cheese)
12 basil leaves
60 ml (2 fl oz/¼ cup) extra virgin olive oil

Slice the tomato into twelve 1 cm (½ inch) slices. Slice the bocconcini into 24 slices the same thickness as the tomato.

Arrange the tomato slices on a plate, alternating them with two slices of bocconcini and placing a basil leaf between the bocconcini slices.

Drizzle with the olive oil and season well.

NOTE: You could use whole cherry tomatoes and toss them with the bocconcini and basil.

# Prawn and Cucumber Salad

🌺 SERVES 4

🌺 PREPARATION TIME: 20 MINUTES

🌺 COOKING TIME: 5 MINUTES

1 Lebanese (short) cucumber, peeled
375 g (13 oz) raw prawns (shrimp)
60 ml (2 fl oz/¼ cup) rice vinegar
1 tablespoon caster (superfine) sugar
1 tablespoon Japanese soy sauce
1 teaspoon finely grated fresh ginger
1 tablespoon white sesame seeds, toasted

Halve the cucumber lengthways and remove the seeds. Cut into thin slices, sprinkle thoroughly with salt and set aside for 5 minutes. Rinse to remove the salt and pat dry with paper towels. Put the prawns in a saucepan of lightly salted boiling water and simmer for 2 minutes, or until just cooked. Drain, then plunge them into cold water. When the prawns are cool, peel them, leaving the tails intact. Gently pull out the dark vein from each prawn back, starting at the head end.

Put the vinegar, sugar, soy sauce and ginger in a large bowl and stir until the sugar dissolves. Add the prawns and cucumber, cover and marinate in the refrigerator for 1 hour.

Drain the prawns and cucumber from the marinade. Arrange on serving plates, sprinkle with the sesame seeds and serve.

*Tomato and Bocconcini Salad*

# Stuffed Artichokes

❀ SERVES 6

❀ PREPARATION TIME: 1 HOUR 30 MINUTES

❀ COOKING TIME: 1 HOUR 25 MINUTES

125 ml (4 fl oz/$^{1}/_{2}$ cup) lemon juice

12 globe artichokes

500 g (1 lb 2 oz) minced (ground) lamb

40 g (1$^{1}/_{2}$ oz/$^{1}/_{2}$ cup) fresh breadcrumbs

1 egg, lightly beaten

1 tablespoon chopped thyme

olive oil, for deep-frying

125 ml (4 fl oz/$^{1}/_{2}$ cup) extra virgin olive
    oil

$^{1}/_{2}$ teaspoon ground turmeric

1 bay leaf

375 ml (13 fl oz/1$^{1}/_{2}$ cups) chicken stock

40 g (1$^{1}/_{2}$ oz) butter

2 tablespoons plain (all-purpose) flour

Fill a large bowl with water and add 60 ml (2 fl oz/ $^{1}/_{4}$ cup) of the lemon juice. Peel the outer leaves from the artichokes, trimming the stems to reveal the bases. Cut the tops off to reveal the chokes and remove the chokes. Put the artichokes in the bowl of acidulated water.

Put the lamb, breadcrumbs, egg and thyme in a bowl, season and mix well. Pat the artichokes dry with paper towels and fill each with 2 tablespoons of the lamb mixture.

Fill a deep-fryer or heavy-based saucepan one-third full of olive oil and heat to 180°C (350°F), or until a cube of bread dropped into the oil browns in 15 seconds. Cook the artichokes in batches for 5 minutes, or until golden brown. Drain well.

Put the extra virgin olive oil, turmeric, bay leaf, remaining lemon juice and 250 ml (9 fl oz/1 cup) of the stock in a 1.25 litre (44 fl oz/5-cup) flameproof casserole dish. Season, then bring to the boil. Add the artichokes, reduce the heat, cover and simmer for 1 hour, or until tender, adding more stock if necessary. Turn the artichokes twice during cooking. Remove the artichokes and keep warm. Reserve the cooking liquid.

Melt the butter in a saucepan, add the flour and stir for 1 minute, or until pale and foamy. Remove from the heat and gradually stir in the reserved cooking liquid. Return to the heat and stir until the sauce boils and thickens, then reduce the heat and simmer for 2 minutes. Serve immediately with the artichokes.

# Fast Melon Salad

❁ SERVES 4–6
❁ PREPARATION TIME: 15 MINUTES
❁ COOKING TIME: NIL

1 large honeydew melon
60 g (2¼ oz/2 cups) watercress sprigs,
    trimmed
2 avocados, sliced
1 large red capsicum (pepper), thinly sliced
220 g (7¾ oz) marinated feta cheese,
    crumbled into large chunks
90 g (3¼ oz) marinated niçoise olives

DRESSING
60 ml (2 fl oz/¼ cup) olive oil
2 tablespoons white wine vinegar
1 teaspoon dijon mustard

Cut the honeydew melon into slices and arrange on a large platter. Scatter the watercress sprigs over the top. Arrange the avocado, capsicum, feta cheese and niçoise olives on top.

To make the dressing, put the oil, vinegar and mustard in a screw-top jar and shake until well combined. Drizzle over the salad.

# Chef's Salad

❁ SERVES 4
❁ PREPARATION TIME: 25 MINUTES
❁ COOKING TIME: NIL

DRESSING
125 ml (4 fl oz/½ cup) extra virgin
    olive oil
2 tablespoons white wine vinegar
1 teaspoon sugar

1 iceberg lettuce
2 tomatoes, cut into wedges
2 celery stalks, cut into thin batons
1 cooked boneless, skinless chicken breast,
    cut into thin strips
200 g (7 oz) ham, cut into thin strips
60 g (2¼ oz) Swiss cheese, cut into strips
3 hard-boiled eggs, cut into wedges
6 radishes, sliced

Whisk the dressing ingredients together in a bowl until well combined. Season to taste.

Roughly shred the lettuce leaves and divide among serving plates. Top with layers of the tomato, celery, chicken, ham, cheese, egg and radish. Drizzle the dressing over the salad and serve immediately.

*Fast Melon Salad*

# Salmon and Fennel Salad

* SERVES 4
* PREPARATION TIME: 15 MINUTES
* COOKING TIME: NIL

2 fennel bulbs
2 teaspoons dijon mustard
1 teaspoon caster (superfine) sugar
125 ml (4 fl oz/½ cup) olive oil
2 tablespoons lemon juice
200 g (7 oz) smoked salmon, cut into
    strips
2 tablespoons snipped chives
1 tablespoon chopped dill (optional)
rocket (arugula), to serve

Trim the fronds from the fennel. Slice the fennel bulbs and chop the fronds.

To make the dressing, whisk together the mustard, sugar, olive oil and lemon juice in a large bowl.

Add the sliced fennel bulb, salmon, chives and 1 tablespoon fennel fronds or dill to the bowl. Season and toss gently. Serve with the rocket and some toast.

# Stuffed Mushrooms

* SERVES 4
* PREPARATION TIME: 10 MINUTES
* COOKING TIME: 25 MINUTES

8 large cap mushrooms
80 ml (2½ fl oz/⅓ cup) olive oil
30 g (1 oz) prosciutto, finely chopped
1 garlic clove, crushed
2 tablespoons soft fresh breadcrumbs
30 g (1 oz) freshly grated parmesan
    cheese
2 tablespoons chopped flat-leaf (Italian)
    parsley

Preheat the oven to 190°C (375°F/Gas 5). Lightly grease a baking dish. Remove the mushroom stalks and finely chop them.

Heat 1 tablespoon of the oil in a frying pan, add the prosciutto, garlic and mushroom stalks and cook for 5 minutes. Mix in a bowl with the breadcrumbs, parmesan and parsley.

Brush the mushroom caps with 1 tablespoon of the olive oil and place them, gill side up, on the baking dish. Divide the stuffing among the caps and bake for 20 minutes. Drizzle with the remaining oil and serve hot or warm.

*Salmon and Fennel Salad*

# Russian Salad

❁ SERVES 4–6
❁ PREPARATION TIME: 40 MINUTES
❁ COOKING TIME: 40 MINUTES

MAYONNAISE
2 egg yolks
1 teaspoon dijon mustard
125 ml (4 fl oz/½ cup) extra virgin olive
    oil
2 tablespoons lemon juice
2 small garlic cloves, crushed

3 tinned globe artichoke hearts
3 waxy potatoes, such as desiree, unpeeled
100 g (3½ oz) baby green beans, trimmed
    and cut into 1 cm (½ inch) lengths
1 large carrot, cut into 1 cm (½ inch)
    cubes
125 g (4½ oz) fresh peas
30 g (1 oz) cornichons, chopped
2 tablespoons baby capers, rinsed and
    drained
4 anchovy fillets, finely chopped
10 black olives, cut into 3 slices
black olives, to garnish

To make the mayonnaise, beat the egg yolks with the mustard and ¼ teaspoon salt using electric beaters until creamy. Gradually add the oil in a fine stream, beating constantly until all the oil has been added. Add the lemon juice, garlic and 1 teaspoon boiling water and beat for 1 minute until well combined. Season, to taste.

Cut each artichoke into quarters. Rinse the potatoes, cover with cold salted water and bring to a gentle simmer. Cook for 15–20 minutes, or until tender when pierced with a knife. Drain and allow to cool slightly. Peel and set aside. When the potatoes are completely cool, cut into 1 cm (½ inch) cubes.

Blanch the beans in boiling salted water until tender but still firm to the bite. Refresh in cold water, then drain thoroughly. Repeat with the carrot and peas.

Set aside a small quantity of each vegetable, including the cornichons, for the garnish and season, to taste. Put the remainder in a bowl with the capers, anchovies and sliced olives. Add the mayonnaise, toss to combine and season to taste. Arrange on a serving dish and garnish with the reserved vegetables and the whole olives.

NOTE: This salad can be prepared up to 2 days in advance and stored in the refrigerator but should be served at room temperature.

# Asparagus with Citrus Hollandaise

❋ SERVES 4
❋ PREPARATION TIME: 15 MINUTES
❋ COOKING TIME: 8 MINUTES

24 asparagus spears, woody ends trimmed
185 g (6½ oz) butter
4 egg yolks
1–2 tablespoons lemon, lime or
    orange juice
shavings of parmesan or pecorino
    cheese (optional)

Put the asparagus in a saucepan of boiling water. Simmer for 2–4 minutes, or until just tender. Drain well.

Melt the butter in a small saucepan. Skim any froth from the top and discard. Allow the butter to cool.

Combine the egg yolks and 2 tablespoons water in a small saucepan and whisk for 30 seconds, or until pale and creamy. Place the pan over very low heat and continue whisking for 3 minutes, or until the mixture thickens. Remove from the heat. Add the cooled butter gradually, whisking constantly (leave the whey in the bottom of the pan). Stir in the lemon, lime or orange juice and season to taste. Drizzle the sauce over the asparagus and garnish with cheese shavings (if desired).

# Mixed Vegetable Salad

❋ SERVES 4–6
❋ PREPARATION TIME: 40 MINUTES
❋ COOKING TIME: 5 MINUTES

300 g (10½ oz) pineapple, chopped
1 telegraph (long) cucumber, chopped
250 g (9 oz) cherry tomatoes, halved
155 g (5½ oz) green beans, thinly sliced
155 g (5½ oz) bean sprouts, trimmed
80 ml (2½ fl oz/⅓ cup) rice vinegar
2 tablespoons lime juice
2 red chillies, seeded and very finely
    chopped
2 teaspoons sugar
30 g (1 oz) dried shrimp, to garnish
small mint leaves, to garnish

Toss together the pineapple, cucumber, tomatoes, beans and sprouts in a bowl. Cover and refrigerate until chilled. Combine the vinegar, lime juice, chilli and sugar in a small bowl and stir until the sugar dissolves.

Dry-fry the shrimp in a frying pan, shaking the pan constantly until the shrimp are light orange and fragrant. Process the shrimp in a food processor until finely chopped.

Arrange the chilled salad on a serving platter, drizzle the dressing over the top and garnish with the chopped shrimp and mint leaves. Serve immediately.

*Asparagus with Citrus Hollandaise*

# Fish and Herb Salad

🌺 SERVES 4–6

🌺 PREPARATION TIME: 40 MINUTES

🌺 COOKING TIME: 15 MINUTES

500 g (1 lb 2 oz) smoked cod

60 ml (2 fl oz/¼ cup) lime juice

30 g (1 oz/½ cup) flaked coconut

200 g (7 oz/1 cup) jasmine rice, cooked
    and cooled

25 g (1 oz) Vietnamese mint, chopped

3 tablespoons chopped mint

25 g (1 oz) chopped coriander (cilantro)
    leaves

8 makrut (kaffir lime) leaves, very finely
    shredded

DRESSING

1 tablespoon chopped coriander
    (cilantro) root

2 cm (¾ inch) piece fresh ginger, finely
    grated

1 red chilli, finely chopped

1 tablespoon chopped lemon grass, white
    part only

3 tablespoons chopped Thai basil

1 avocado, chopped

80 ml (2½ fl oz/⅓ cup) lime juice

2 tablespoons fish sauce

1 teaspoon soft brown sugar

125 ml (4 fl oz/½ cup) peanut oil

Preheat the oven to 150°C (300°F/Gas 2). Put the cod in a large frying pan and cover with water. Add the lime juice and simmer for 15 minutes, or until the fish flakes when tested with a fork. Drain and set aside to cool slightly before breaking it into bite-sized pieces.

Meanwhile, spread the coconut onto a baking tray and toast in the oven for 10 minutes, or until golden brown, shaking the tray occasionally. Remove the coconut from the tray to prevent it burning.

Put the fish, coconut, rice, Vietnamese mint, mint, coriander and makrut leaves in a large bowl and mix to combine.

To make the dressing, put the coriander root, ginger, chilli, lemon grass and basil in a food processor and process until combined. Add the avocado, lime juice, fish sauce, sugar and peanut oil and process until creamy. Pour the dressing over the salad and toss to coat the rice and fish. Serve immediately.

# Haloumi with Salad and Garlic Bread

☙ SERVES 4
☙ PREPARATION TIME: 20 MINUTES
☙ COOKING TIME: 5 MINUTES

4 firm tomatoes
1 Lebanese (short) cucumber
140 g (5 oz/4 cups) rocket (arugula)
95 g (3¼ oz/½ cup) kalamata olives
1 loaf crusty unsliced white bread
100 ml (3½ fl oz) olive oil
1 large garlic clove, halved
400 g (14 oz) haloumi cheese
1 tablespoon lemon juice
1 tablespoon chopped oregano, plus a few
    small whole leaves to garnish

Preheat the oven to 180°C (350°F/Gas 4). Heat the grill (broiler) to high.

Cut the tomatoes and cucumber into bite-sized chunks and place in a serving dish with the rocket and olives. Mix well.

Slice the bread into eight 1.5 cm (⅝ inch) slices, drizzle 1½ tablespoons of the olive oil over the bread and season. Grill until lightly golden, then rub each slice thoroughly with a cut side of the garlic. Wrap loosely in foil and keep warm in the oven.

Cut the haloumi into eight slices. Heat 2 teaspoons of the oil in a shallow frying pan and fry the haloumi slices for 1–2 minutes each side, or until crisp and golden brown.

Whisk together the lemon juice, oregano and remaining olive oil to make a dressing. Season to taste. Pour half the dressing over the salad and toss well. Arrange the haloumi on top and drizzle with the remaining dressing. Serve immediately with the garlic bread.

# Crab and Mango Salad

❀ SERVES 4
❀ PREPARATION TIME: 25 MINUTES
❀ COOKING TIME: 5 MINUTES

DRESSING
80 ml (2½ fl oz/⅓ cup) light olive oil
60 ml (2 fl oz/¼ cup) lime juice
1 teaspoon fish sauce
½ small green chilli, finely chopped
1 tablespoon finely chopped coriander
    (cilantro) leaves
2 teaspoons grated fresh ginger

2 x 4 cm (1½ inch) squares fresh coconut
1 teaspoon olive oil
60 g (2¼ oz/2 cups) watercress, trimmed
100 g (3½ oz) snow pea (mangetout)
    sprouts
100 g (3½ oz) small cooked prawns
    (shrimp)
400 g (14 oz) cooked fresh or tinned
    crabmeat, drained if tinned
1 firm mango, cut into thin strips
coriander (cilantro) leaves, to garnish
1 lime, cut into slices, to garnish

To make the dressing, combine all the ingredients and season. Set aside to allow the flavours to infuse.

Peel the coconut into wafer-thin slices with a vegetable peeler. Heat the olive oil in a frying pan and gently fry the coconut, stirring, until golden. Drain on crumpled paper towels.

Combine the watercress and snow pea sprouts and arrange on a platter.

Peel the prawns, leaving the tails intact. Gently pull out the dark vein from each prawn back, starting at the head end. Lightly toss the crabmeat, prawns, mango and three-quarters of the toasted coconut and the dressing together. Pile in the centre of the watercress and snow pea sprout mixture, scatter the remaining coconut over the top and garnish with the coriander leaves and lime slices.

NOTE: If you can't get fresh coconut, use 30 g (1 oz/½ cup) flaked coconut and toast it.

# Gado Gado

🌿 SERVES 6–8
🌿 PREPARATION TIME: 30 MINUTES
🌿 COOKING TIME: 35 MINUTES

6 new potatoes
2 carrots, cut into batons
250 g (9 oz) snake (yard-long) beans,
    trimmed and cut into 10 cm (4 inch)
    lengths
2 tablespoons peanut oil
250 g (9 oz) firm tofu, cubed
100 g (3½ oz) baby English spinach leaves
2 Lebanese (short) cucumbers, cut into
    thick strips
1 large red capsicum (pepper), cut into
    thick strips
100 g (3½ oz) bean sprouts, trimmed
5 hard-boiled eggs, cut in half

PEANUT SAUCE
1 tablespoon peanut oil
1 onion, finely chopped
160 g (5¾ oz/⅔ cup) peanut butter
60 ml (2 fl oz/¼ cup) kecap manis
2 tablespoons ground coriander
2 teaspoons chilli sauce
185 ml (6 fl oz/¾ cup) coconut cream
1 teaspoon grated palm sugar (jaggery) or
    soft brown sugar
1 tablespoon lemon juice

Cook the potatoes in a saucepan of salted boiling water until tender. Drain, cool slightly, then cut into quarters.

Cook the carrots and beans separately until just tender. Drain, plunge into iced water, then drain thoroughly.

Heat the oil in a non-stick frying pan and cook the tofu all over in batches until crisp. Drain on crumpled paper towels.

To make the peanut sauce, heat the oil in a frying pan over low heat and cook the onion for 5 minutes, or until golden. Add the peanut butter, kecap manis, coriander, chilli sauce and coconut cream. Bring to the boil, reduce the heat and simmer for 5 minutes. Stir in the sugar and lemon juice, stirring until dissolved.

Arrange all the vegetables, tofu and eggs on a plate around the bowl of peanut sauce.

# Caesar Salad

🌼 SERVES 6
🌼 PREPARATION TIME: 25 MINUTES
🌼 COOKING TIME: 20 MINUTES

1 small baguette
2 tablespoons olive oil
2 garlic cloves, halved
4 bacon slices (trimmed of fat)
2 cos (romaine) lettuces
10 anchovy fillets, halved lengthways
100 g (3½ oz/1 cup) shaved parmesan
    cheese
parmesan cheese shavings, extra, to serve

DRESSING
1 egg yolk
2 garlic cloves, crushed
2 teaspoons dijon mustard
2 anchovy fillets
2 tablespoons white wine vinegar
1 tablespoon worcestershire sauce
185 ml (6 fl oz/¾ cup) olive oil

Preheat the oven to 180°C (350°F/Gas 4). To make the croutons, cut the baguette into 15 thin slices and brush both sides of each slice with oil. Spread them on a baking tray and bake for 10–15 minutes, or until golden brown. Leave to cool slightly, then rub each side of each slice with the cut edge of a garlic clove. The baked bread can then be broken roughly into pieces or cut into small cubes.

Cook the bacon under a hot grill (broiler) until crisp. Drain on paper towels until cooled, then break into chunky pieces.

Tear the lettuce into pieces and put in a serving bowl with the bacon, anchovies, croutons and parmesan.

To make the dressing, place the egg yolk, garlic, mustard, anchovies, vinegar and worcestershire sauce in a food processor or blender. Season and process for 20 seconds, or until smooth. With the motor running, add enough oil in a thin stream to make the dressing thick and creamy.

Drizzle the dressing over the salad and toss very gently until well distributed. Sprinkle the extra parmesan shavings over the top.

# Nachos with Guacamole

❋ SERVES 4
❋ PREPARATION TIME: 20 MINUTES
❋ COOKING TIME: 5 MINUTES

440 g (15½ oz) tinned red kidney beans,
   rinsed and drained
90 g (3¼ oz/⅓ cup) ready-made
   tomato salsa
250 g (9 oz) corn chips
250 g (9 oz/2 cups) grated cheddar cheese
375 g (13 oz/1½ cups) ready-made
   tomato salsa, extra
90 g (3¼ oz/⅓ cup) sour cream

GUACAMOLE
1 spring onion (scallion)
1 small tomato
1 large avocado
1 tablespoon lemon juice

Preheat the oven to 180°C (350°F/Gas 4). Combine the kidney beans and salsa, then divide the mixture between four ovenproof serving plates. Cover with corn chips and grated cheese. Put in the oven for 3–5 minutes, or until the cheese has melted.

To assemble, spoon the extra salsa onto the melted cheese, then top with guacamole and sour cream.

To make the guacamole, finely chop the spring onion and tomato. Cut the avocado in half, discard the skin and stone. Mash the flesh lightly with a fork and combine with the spring onion, tomato, lemon juice and some freshly ground pepper.

# Duck and Watercress Salad with Lychees

🌸 SERVES 4

🌸 PREPARATION TIME: 25 MINUTES

🌸 COOKING TIME: 30 MINUTES

2 large duck breasts, skin on
1 tablespoon soy sauce
1/2 each red, green and yellow capsicum
    (pepper)
250 g (9 oz) watercress
12 fresh or canned lychees
2 tablespoons pickled shredded ginger
1–2 tablespoons green peppercorns
    (optional)
1 tablespoon white wine vinegar
2 teaspoons soft brown sugar
1–2 teaspoons chopped red chilli
1 large handful coriander (cilantro) leaves

Preheat the oven to 210°C (415°F/Gas 6–7). Brush the duck breasts with the soy sauce and put on a rack in a baking tin. Bake for 30 minutes. Remove from the oven and allow to cool.

Slice the capsicums into thin strips. Discard any tough woody stems from the watercress. Peel the fresh lychees and remove the seeds. If you are using canned lychees, drain them thoroughly.

Arrange the capsicum strips, watercress, lychees and ginger on a large serving platter. Slice the duck into thin pieces and toss gently through the salad.

In a small bowl, combine the peppercorns, if using, vinegar, sugar, chilli and coriander. Serve this on the side for spooning over the salad.

# Prosciutto, Camembert and Fig Salad

🌸 SERVES 4

🌸 PREPARATION TIME: 10 MINUTES

🌸 COOKING TIME: 5 MINUTES

60 g (2¼ oz) thinly sliced prosciutto
1 curly oak leaf lettuce
4 fresh figs, quartered
100 g (3½ oz) camembert cheese,
    thinly sliced
1 garlic clove, crushed
1 tablespoon mustard
2 tablespoons white wine vinegar
80 ml (2½ fl oz/⅓ cup) olive oil

Grill (broil) the prosciutto until crisp.

Arrange the lettuce leaves on a large plate and top with the figs, camembert and prosciutto.

Whisk together the garlic, mustard, vinegar and olive oil and drizzle over the salad.

*Watercress and Duck Salad with Lychees*

# Green Papaya Salad

🌸 SERVES 6

🌸 PREPARATION TIME: 25 MINUTES

🌸 COOKING TIME: 5 MINUTES

370 g (13 oz) green papaya, peeled and
    seeded
90 g (3¼ oz) snake (yard-long) beans,
    trimmed and cut into 2 cm (¾ inch)
    lengths
2 garlic cloves
2 small red chillies, chopped
5 teaspoons dried shrimp
8 cherry tomatoes, halved
50 g (1¾ oz) coriander (cilantro) sprigs
40 g (1½ oz/¼ cup) chopped roasted
    peanuts
1 small red chili, sliced (optional)

DRESSING
60 ml (2 fl oz/¼ cup) fish sauce
2 tablespoons tamarind purée
1 tablespoon lime juice
3 tablespoons grated palm sugar (jaggery)

Grate the papaya, sprinkle with salt and leave for
30 minutes. Rinse well.

Cook the beans in a saucepan of boiling water for
3 minutes, or until tender. Drain, plunge into cold
water, then drain again.

To make the dressing, combine all ingredients in a
small bowl. Set aside.

Pound the garlic and chilli using a large mortar and
pestle until crushed. Add the dried shrimp and pound
until puréed. Add the papaya and snake beans and
lightly pound for 1 minute. Add the tomato and pound
briefly to bruise.

Combine the coriander with the papaya mixture and
spoon onto serving plates. Pour the dressing over the
top. Sprinkle with the peanuts and, if desired, sliced
red chilli.

# Cold Vegetable Salad with Spice Dressing

300 g (10½ oz) green or snake
   (yard-long) beans
10 English spinach leaves
80 g (2¾ oz) snow pea (mangetout)
   sprouts
1 red capsicum (pepper)
1 red onion
100 g (3½ oz) bean sprouts, trimmed

SPICE DRESSING
2 tablespoons peanut oil
1 garlic clove, crushed
1 teaspoon grated fresh ginger
1 small red chilli, chopped
2 tablespoons desiccated coconut
1 tablespoon brown vinegar

Top and tail the beans and cut them into 10 cm (4 inch) lengths. Remove the stems from the spinach leaves and slice the leaves thinly. Remove about 1 cm (½ inch) of the long stems from the snow pea sprouts. Cut the capsicum into thin strips. Thinly slice the onion.

Put the beans in a large saucepan of boiling water and cook for 1 minute to blanch, then drain. Combine the beans, spinach, snow pea sprouts, bean sprouts, capsicum and onion in a bowl.

To make the spice dressing, heat the oil in a small frying pan. Add the garlic, ginger, chilli and coconut, and stir-fry over medium heat for 1 minute. Add the vinegar and 80 ml (2½ fl oz/⅓ cup) water, and simmer for 1 minute. Allow to cool.

To serve, add the dressing to the vegetables, and toss until combined.

NOTES: Snow pea (mangetout) sprouts are the growing tips and tendrils from the snow pea plant.
   Any blanched vegetables can be used in this salad. Try to use a variety of vegetables which result in a colourful appearance.
   The spice dressing can be added up to 30 minutes before serving.

# Pork Noodle Salad

❀ SERVES 4–6

❀ PREPARATION TIME: 20 MINUTES

❀ COOKING TIME: 35 MINUTES

BROTH

250 ml (9 fl oz/1 cup) chicken stock

3 coriander (cilantro) roots

2 makrut (kaffir lime) leaves

3 cm (1¼ inch) piece fresh ginger, sliced

100 g (3½ oz) dried rice vermicelli

30 g (1 oz) wood ear fungus (see Note)

1 small red chilli, seeded and thinly sliced

2 red Asian shallots, thinly sliced

2 spring onions (scallions), thinly sliced

2 garlic cloves, crushed

250 g (9 oz) minced (ground) pork

60 ml (2 fl oz/¼ cup) lime juice

60 ml (2 fl oz/¼ cup) fish sauce

1½ tablespoons grated palm sugar
   (jaggery)

¼ teaspoon ground white pepper

1 large handful coriander (cilantro) leaves,
   chopped

oakleaf or coral lettuce, to serve

lime wedges, to garnish

chilli strips, to garnish

coriander (cilantro) leaves, extra,
   to garnish

To make the broth, combine the stock, coriander roots, makrut leaves, ginger and 250 ml (9 fl oz/1 cup) water in a saucepan. Simmer for 25 minutes, or until the liquid has reduced to 185 ml (6 fl oz/¾ cup). Strain and return to the pan.

Soak the vermicelli in a saucepan of boiling water for 6–7 minutes. Drain, then cut into 3 cm (1¼ inch) lengths. Discard the woody stems from the wood ear, then thinly slice. Combine the vermicelli, wood ear, chilli, shallot, spring onion and garlic.

Return the broth to the heat and bring to the boil. Add the pork and stir, breaking up any lumps, for 1–2 minutes, or until the pork changes colour and is cooked. Drain, then add to the vermicelli mixture.

In a separate bowl, combine the lime juice, fish sauce, palm sugar and white pepper, stirring until the sugar has dissolved. Add to the pork mixture along with the coriander and mix well. Season with salt.

To assemble, tear or shred the lettuce, then arrange on a serving dish. Spoon the pork and noodle mixture on the lettuce and garnish with the lime wedges, chilli and extra coriander.

NOTE: Wood ear (also called black fungus) is a cultivated wood fungus. It is mainly available dried; and needs to be reconstituted in boiling water for a few minutes until it expands to five times its dried size, before cooking.

# Panzanella

✿ SERVES 6–8

✿ PREPARATION TIME: 30 MINUTES

✿ COOKING TIME: 5 MINUTES

1 small red onion, thinly sliced

250 g (9 oz) stale bread such as ciabatta,
    crusts removed

4 ripe tomatoes

6 anchovy fillets, finely chopped

1 small garlic clove, crushed

1 tablespoon baby capers, rinsed, squeezed
    dry and chopped

2 tablespoons red wine vinegar

125 ml (4 fl oz/$\frac{1}{2}$ cup) extra virgin
    olive oil

2 small Lebanese (short) cucumbers,
    peeled and sliced

30 g (1 oz) basil leaves, torn

In a small bowl, cover the onion with cold water and leave for 5 minutes. Squeeze the rings in your hand, closing tightly and letting go and repeating that process about five times. This removes the acid from the onion. Repeat the whole process twice more, using fresh water each time.

Tear the bread into rough 3 cm (1$\frac{1}{4}$ inch) squares and toast lightly under a grill (broiler) for 4 minutes, or until bread is crisp but not browned. Allow to cool. Set aside.

Score a cross in the base of each tomato. Put in a heatproof bowl and cover with boiling water. Leave for 30 seconds, then transfer to cold water, drain and peel away the skin from the cross. Cut each tomato in half and scoop out the seeds. Roughly chop two of the tomatoes and purée the other two.

Combine the anchovies, garlic and capers in a bowl. Add the vinegar and olive oil and whisk to combine. Season, then transfer to a large bowl and add the bread, onion, puréed and chopped tomato, cucumber and basil. Toss well and season, to taste. Leave to stand for at least 15 minutes to allow the flavours to develop. Serve at room temperature.

# Frisée and Garlic Crouton Salad

❀ SERVES 4–6
❀ PREPARATION TIME: 20 MINUTES
❀ COOKING TIME: 10 MINUTES

VINAIGRETTE
1 French shallot, finely chopped
1 tablespoon dijon mustard
60 ml (2 fl oz/¼ cup) tarragon vinegar
170 ml (5½ fl oz/²⁄₃ cup) extra virgin
    olive oil

1 tablespoon olive oil
250 g (9 oz) speck, rind removed, cut into
    5 mm x 2 cm (¼ x ¾ inch) pieces
½ baguette, sliced
4 garlic cloves
1 baby frisée (curly endive)
100 g (3½ oz) walnuts, toasted

To make the vinaigrette, whisk together the shallot, mustard and vinegar in a small bowl. Slowly add the oil, whisking constantly until thickened. Set aside.

Heat the oil in a large frying pan, add the speck, bread and garlic and cook over medium–high heat for 5–8 minutes, or until the bread and speck are both crisp. Remove the garlic from the pan.

Put the frisée, baguette, speck, walnuts and vinaigrette in a large bowl. Toss together well and serve.

# Tuna, Green Bean and Onion Salad

❀ SERVES 4
❀ PREPARATION TIME: 20 MINUTES
❀ COOKING TIME: 15 MINUTES

200 g (7 oz) green beans, trimmed and
    cut into short lengths
300 g (10½ oz) penne rigate
125 ml (4 fl oz/½ cup) olive oil
250 g (9 oz) tuna steak, cut into thick
    slices
1 red onion, thinly sliced
1 tablespoon balsamic vinegar

In a large saucepan of boiling water, cook the beans for 1–2 minutes, or until tender but still crisp. Remove with a slotted spoon and rinse under cold water. Drain and transfer to a serving bowl.

Cook the pasta in a saucepan of boiling salted water until *al dente*. Drain, rinse under cold water and drain again before adding to the beans.

Heat half the oil in a frying pan. Add the tuna and onion and gently sauté until the tuna is just cooked through. Stir the tuna carefully to prevent it from breaking up. Add the vinegar, increase the heat to high and briefly cook until the dressing has reduced and lightly coats the tuna. Transfer the tuna and onion to a bowl.

Toss the beans, pasta, tuna and onion together and mix with the remaining oil, and season to taste. Allow to cool before serving.

# Prawn and Papaya Salad with Lime Dressing

❧ SERVES 4
❧ PREPARATION TIME: 25 MINUTES
❧ COOKING TIME: NIL

750 g (1 lb 10 oz) cooked prawns
    (shrimp)
1 large papaya, chopped
1 small red onion, thinly sliced
2 celery stalks, thinly sliced
2 tablespoons shredded mint

LIME DRESSING
125 ml (4 fl oz/½ cup) vegetable oil
60 ml (2 fl oz/¼ cup) lime juice
2 teaspoons finely grated fresh ginger
1 teaspoon caster (superfine) sugar

Peel the prawns, leaving the tails intact. Gently pull out the dark vein from each prawn back, starting from the head end. Put the prawns in a bowl.

To make the lime dressing, put the oil, lime juice, ginger and sugar in a small bowl and whisk to combine. Season well.

Add the lime dressing to the prawns and gently toss to coat the prawns. Add the papaya, onion, celery and mint and gently toss to combine. Serve the salad at room temperature, or cover and refrigerate for up to 3 hours before serving.

# Fresh Beetroot and Goat's Cheese Salad

❧ SERVES 4
❧ PREPARATION TIME: 20 MINUTES
❧ COOKING TIME: 30 MINUTES

1 kg (2 lb 4 oz) fresh beetroot (beets)
    (about 4 bulbs) with leaves
200 g (7 oz) green beans, trimmed
1 tablespoon red wine vinegar
2 tablespoons extra virgin olive oil
1 garlic clove, crushed
1 tablespoon capers, rinsed and squeezed
    dry, roughly chopped
100 g (3½ oz) goat's cheese

Trim the leaves from the beetroot, scrub the bulbs and wash the leaves. Put the bulbs in a large saucepan of salted water, bring to the boil, then reduce the heat, cover and simmer for 30 minutes, or until tender. Drain and cool the bulbs, peel the skins off and cut into thin wedges.

Meanwhile, bring a saucepan of water to the boil, add the beans and cook for 3 minutes, or until just tender. Remove with a slotted spoon and plunge into a bowl of cold water. Drain well. Add the beetroot leaves to the same pan of water and cook for 3–5 minutes, or until the leaves and stems are tender. Drain, plunge into a bowl of cold water, then drain well.

To make the dressing, mix the vinegar, oil, garlic, capers and ½ teaspoon each of salt and pepper. Divide the beans, beetroot leaves and bulbs among four serving plates. Crumble the goat's cheese over the top of each and drizzle with dressing.

*Prawn and Papaya Salad with Lime Dressing*

# Chilled Soba Noodles

SERVES 4
PREPARATION TIME: 25 MINUTES
COOKING TIME: 15 MINUTES

250 g (9 oz) dried soba (buckwheat) noodles
4 cm ($1\frac{1}{2}$ inch) piece fresh ginger
1 carrot
4 spring onions (scallions), outside layer removed
1 sheet nori, to garnish
pickled ginger, to garnish
thinly sliced pickled daikon, to garnish

DIPPING SAUCE
3 tablespoons dashi granules
125 ml (4 fl oz/$\frac{1}{2}$ cup) Japanese soy sauce
80 ml ($2\frac{1}{2}$ fl oz/$\frac{1}{3}$ cup) mirin

Put the noodles in a large saucepan of boiling water. When the water returns to the boil, pour in 250 ml (9 fl oz/1 cup) cold water. Bring the water back to the boil and cook the noodles for 2–3 minutes, or until just tender — take care not to overcook them. Drain the noodles in a colander and then cool under cold running water. Drain thoroughly and set aside.

Cut the ginger and carrot into fine matchsticks about 4 cm ($1\frac{1}{2}$ inches) long. Slice the spring onions very finely. Bring a small saucepan of water to the boil, add the ginger, carrot and spring onion and blanch for about 30 seconds. Drain and place in a bowl of iced water to cool. Drain again when the vegetables are cool.

To make the dipping sauce, combine 375 ml (13 fl oz/ $1\frac{1}{2}$ cups) water, the dashi granules, soy sauce, mirin and a good pinch each of salt and pepper in a small saucepan. Bring the sauce to the boil, then cool completely. When ready to serve, pour the sauce into four small dipping bowls.

Gently toss the cooled noodles and vegetables to combine. Arrange in four individual serving bowls.

Toast the nori by holding it with tongs over low heat and moving it back and forward for about 15 seconds. Cut it into thin strips with scissors, and scatter the strips over the noodles. Place a little pickled ginger and daikon on the side of each plate. Serve the noodles with the dipping sauce. The noodles should be dipped into the sauce before being eaten.

# Tomato and Basil Croustades

❀ SERVES 4
❀ PREPARATION TIME: 30 MINUTES
❀ COOKING TIME: 20 MINUTES

1 day-old white bread loaf

3 tablespoons olive oil

2 garlic cloves, crushed

3 tomatoes, diced

250 g (9 oz) bocconcini (fresh baby mozzarella cheese), cut into small chunks

1 tablespoon tiny capers, rinsed and dried

1 tablespoon extra virgin olive oil

2 teaspoons balsamic vinegar

4 tablespoons shredded basil

Preheat the oven to 180°C (350°F/Gas 4). Remove the crusts from the bread and cut the loaf into four even pieces. Using a small serrated knife, cut a square from the centre of each cube of bread, leaving a border of about 1.5 cm ($^5/_8$ inch) on each side. You should be left with four 'boxes'. Combine the olive oil and garlic and brush all over the croustades. Place them on a baking tray and bake for about 20 minutes, or until golden and crisp. Check them occasionally to make sure they don't burn.

Meanwhile, combine the tomato and bocconcini with the tiny capers in a bowl.

In another bowl, stir together the extra virgin olive oil and balsamic vinegar, then gently toss with the tomato mixture. Season with salt and freshly ground black pepper, then stir in the basil. Spoon into the croustades, allowing any excess to tumble over the sides.

# Thai Beef Salad

🌻 SERVES 6
🌻 PREPARATION TIME: 20 MINUTES
🌻 COOKING TIME: 5 MINUTES

500 g (1 lb 2 oz) lean beef fillet
2 tablespoons peanut oil
2 garlic cloves, crushed
1 tablespoon grated palm sugar (jaggery)
    or soft brown sugar
3 tablespoons finely chopped coriander
    (cilantro) roots and stems
80 ml ($2^{1}/_{2}$ fl oz/$^{1}/_{3}$ cup) lime juice
2 tablespoons fish sauce
$^{1}/_{4}$ teaspoon ground white pepper
2 small red chillies, seeded and thinly
    sliced
2 red Asian shallots, thinly sliced
2 telegraph (long) cucumbers, sliced into
    thin ribbons
2 large handfuls mint
90 g ($3^{1}/_{4}$ oz/1 cup) bean sprouts,
    trimmed
40 g ($1^{1}/_{2}$ oz/$^{1}/_{4}$ cup) chopped roasted
    peanuts

Thinly slice the beef across the grain. Heat a wok over high heat, then add 1 tablespoon of the oil and swirl to coat the side of the wok. Add half the beef and cook for 1–2 minutes, or until medium–rare. Remove from the wok and put on a plate. Repeat with the remaining oil and beef.

Put the garlic, palm or brown sugar, coriander, lime juice, fish sauce, pepper and $^{1}/_{4}$ teaspoon salt in a bowl, and stir until all the sugar has dissolved. Add the chilli and shallots and mix well.

Pour the sauce over the hot beef, mix together well, then allow the beef to cool to room temperature.

In a separate bowl, toss together the cucumber and mint, and refrigerate until required.

Pile up a bed of the cucumber and mint on a serving platter, then top with the beef, bean sprouts and peanuts.

# Vegetable Pakoras

🌸 SERVES 4
🌸 PREPARATION TIME: 30 MINUTES
🌸 COOKING TIME: 20 MINUTES

RAITA
2 Lebanese (short) cucumbers, peeled,
    seeded and finely chopped
250 g (9 oz/1 cup) plain yoghurt
1 teaspoon ground cumin
1 teaspoon mustard seeds
1/2 teaspoon grated fresh ginger
paprika, to garnish

35 g (1 1/4 oz/1/3 cup) besan (chickpea
    flour)
40 g (1 1/2 oz/1/3 cup) self-raising flour
45 g (1 3/4 oz/1/3 cup) soy flour
1/2 teaspoon ground turmeric
1 teaspoon cayenne pepper
1/2 teaspoon ground coriander
1 small green chilli, seeded and finely
    chopped
200 g (7 oz) cauliflower
140 g (5 oz) orange sweet potato
180 g (6 1/4 oz) eggplant (aubergine)
180 g (6 1/4 oz) asparagus, woody ends
    trimmed
vegetable oil, for deep-frying

To make the raita, mix the cucumber and yoghurt in a bowl. Dry-fry the cumin and mustard seeds in a small frying pan over medium heat for 1 minute, or until fragrant and lightly browned, then add to the yoghurt mixture. Stir in the ginger, season to taste and mix together well. Garnish with paprika. Refrigerate until ready to serve.

Sift the besan, self-raising and soy flours into a bowl, then add the turmeric, cayenne pepper, ground coriander, chilli and 1 teaspoon salt. Gradually whisk in 250 ml (9 fl oz/1 cup) cold water until a batter forms. Set aside for 15 minutes. Preheat the oven to 120°C (235°F/Gas 1/2).

Meanwhile, cut the cauliflower into small florets. Cut the sweet potato and eggplant into 5 mm (1/4 inch) slices, and cut the asparagus into 6 cm (2 1/2 inch) lengths.

Fill a wok one-third full with the oil and heat to 170°C (325°F), or until a cube of bread dropped in the oil browns in 20 seconds. Dip the vegetables in the batter, then deep-fry them in small batches, for 1–2 minutes, or until pale golden. Remove with a slotted spoon and drain on crumpled paper towel. Keep warm in the oven until all the vegetables are cooked. Serve with the raita.

seafood

# Oysters with Bloody Mary Sauce

- SERVES 6
- PREPARATION TIME: 20 MINUTES
- COOKING TIME: NIL

24 fresh oysters, on the half shell
60 ml (2 fl oz/¼ cup) tomato juice
2 teaspoons vodka
1 teaspoon lemon juice
½ teaspoon worcestershire sauce
1–2 drops of Tabasco sauce
1 celery stalk
1–2 teaspoons snipped chives

Remove the oysters from their shells. Clean and dry the shells. Combine the tomato juice, vodka, lemon juice, worcestershire sauce and Tabasco sauce in a small bowl.

Cut the celery into very thin julienne strips and place in the bases of the oyster shells. Top with an oyster and drizzle with tomato mixture. Sprinkle with snipped chives.

# Gravlax with Mustard Sauce

- SERVES 12
- PREPARATION TIME: 10 MINUTES
- COOKING TIME: NIL

55 g (2 oz/¼ cup) sugar
2 tablespoons sea salt
1 teaspoon crushed black peppercorns
2.5 kg (5 lb 8 oz) salmon, filleted, skin on, cut into 2 fillets
1 tablespoon vodka or brandy
4 tablespoons very finely chopped dill

MUSTARD SAUCE
1½ tablespoons cider vinegar
1 teaspoon caster (superfine) sugar
125 ml (4 fl oz/½ cup) olive oil
2 teaspoons chopped dill
2 tablespoons dijon mustard

Combine the sugar, salt and peppercorns in a small dish. Remove any bones from the salmon with tweezers. Pat dry with paper towels and lay one fillet, skin-side down, in a shallow tray or ovenproof dish. Sprinkle the fillet with half the vodka, rub half the sugar mixture into the flesh, then sprinkle with half the dill. Sprinkle the remaining vodka over the second fillet and rub the remaining sugar mixture into the flesh. Lay it, flesh-side down, on top of the other fillet. Cover with plastic wrap, place a heavy board on top and then weigh the board down with three heavy tins or a foil-covered brick. Refrigerate for 24 hours, turning it over after 12 hours.

To make the mustard sauce, whisk all the ingredients together, then cover until needed.

Uncover the salmon and lay the fillets on a wooden board. Brush off the dill and seasoning with a stiff pastry brush. Sprinkle with the remaining dill, pressing it onto the salmon flesh, shaking off any excess. Serve whole on the serving board, or thinly sliced on an angle towards the tail, with the sauce.

*NOTE: Gravlax can be refrigerated, covered, for up to a week.*

*Oysters with Bloody Mary Sauce*

# Marinated Seafood

🌺 SERVES 8

🌺 PREPARATION TIME: 40 MINUTES

🌺 COOKING TIME: 10 MINUTES~

500 g (1 lb 2 oz) raw prawns (shrimp)

500 g (1 lb 2 oz) mussels, scrubbed, beards removed

125 ml (4 fl oz/½ cup) white wine vinegar

3 bay leaves

500 g (1 lb 2 oz) small squid tubes, sliced

500 g (1 lb 2 oz) cleaned scallops (without roe)

DRESSING

2 garlic cloves, crushed

125 ml (4 fl oz/½ cup) extra virgin olive oil

60 ml (2 fl oz/¼ cup) lemon juice

1 tablespoon white wine vinegar

1 teaspoon dijon mustard

1 tablespoon chopped flat-leaf (Italian) parsley

Peel the prawns, leaving the tails intact. Gently pull out the dark vein from each prawn back, starting from the head end.

Discard any mussels that are already open. Put the vinegar, bay leaves, 750 ml (26 fl oz/3 cups) water and ½ teaspoon salt in a large saucepan and bring to the boil. Add the squid and scallops, then reduce the heat to low and simmer for 2–3 minutes, or until the seafood has turned white. Remove the squid and scallops with a slotted spoon and put in a bowl.

Repeat the process with the prawns, cooking until just pink, then removing with a slotted spoon. Return the liquid to the boil and add the mussels. Cover, reduce the heat and simmer for 3 minutes, or until all the shells are open. Stir occasionally and discard any unopened mussels. Cool, remove the meat and add to the bowl.

To make the dressing, whisk the garlic and oil together with the lemon juice, vinegar, mustard and parsley. Pour over the seafood and toss well. Refrigerate for 1–2 hours before serving.

*NOTE: Seafood should never be overcooked or it will become tough.*

# Crab Cakes with Avocado Salsa

❁ SERVES 4
❁ PREPARATION TIME: 15 MINUTES
❁ COOKING TIME: 6 MINUTES

2 eggs, lightly beaten
340 g (11¾ oz) tinned crabmeat, drained
1 spring onion (scallion), finely chopped
1 tablespoon mayonnaise
2 teaspoons sweet chilli sauce
100 g (3½ oz/1¼ cups) fresh white
    breadcrumbs
vegetable oil, for pan-frying
lime wedges, to serve
coriander (cilantro) leaves, to garnish

AVOCADO SALSA
2 roma (plum) tomatoes, chopped
1 small red onion, finely chopped
1 large avocado, diced
60 ml (2 fl oz/¼ cup) lime juice
2 tablespoons chervil
1 teaspoon caster (superfine) sugar

Combine the eggs, crabmeat, spring onion, mayonnaise, sweet chilli sauce and breadcrumbs in a bowl. Stir well and season. Using wet hands, form the crab mixture into eight small flat patties. Cover and refrigerate for 30 minutes.

To make the avocado salsa, put the tomato, onion, avocado, lime juice, chervil and sugar in a bowl. Season and toss gently to combine.

Heat the oil in a large heavy-based frying pan to 180°C (350°F), or until a cube of bread dropped into the oil browns in 15 seconds. Cook the crab cakes over medium heat for 6 minutes, or until golden brown on both sides. Drain well on crumpled paper towels. Serve the crab cakes with the bowl of avocado salsa and some lime wedges. Garnish with the coriander leaves.

# Garlic Prawns

❀ SERVES 4
❀ PREPARATION TIME: 20 MINUTES
❀ COOKING TIME: 15 MINUTES

1.25 kg (2 lb 12 oz) raw prawns (shrimp)
80 g (2¾ oz) butter, melted
185 ml (6 fl oz/¾ cup) olive oil
8 garlic cloves, crushed
2 spring onions (scallions), thinly sliced

Preheat the oven to 250°C (500°F/Gas 9). Peel the prawns, leaving the tails intact. Gently pull out the vein from each prawn back, starting at the head end. Cut a slit down the back of each prawn.

Combine the butter and oil and divide among four 500 ml (17 fl oz/2-cup) ovenproof pots. Divide half the crushed garlic among the pots.

Place the pots on a baking tray and heat in the oven for 10 minutes, or until the mixture is bubbling. Divide the prawns and remaining garlic among the pots. Return to the oven for 5 minutes, or until the prawns are cooked. Stir in the spring onion. Season to taste. Serve with bread to mop up the juices.

# Baked Prawns with Feta

❀ SERVES 4
❀ PREPARATION TIME: 20 MINUTES
❀ COOKING TIME: 30 MINUTES

300 g (10½ oz) raw large prawns
    (shrimp)
2 tablespoons olive oil
2 small red onions, finely chopped
1 large garlic clove, crushed
350 g (12 oz) tomatoes, diced
2 tablespoons lemon juice
2 tablespoons fresh oregano or 1 teaspoon
    dried
200 g (7 oz) feta cheese
extra virgin olive oil, for drizzling
chopped flat-leaf (Italian) parsley,
    to garnish

Peel the prawns, leaving the tails intact. Gently pull out the dark vein from each prawn back, starting at the head end.

Preheat the oven to 180°C (350°F/Gas 4). Heat the oil in a saucepan over medium heat, add the onion and cook, stirring occasionally for 3 minutes, or until softened. Add the garlic and cook for a few seconds, then add the tomato and cook for 10 minutes, or until the mixture is slightly reduced and thickened. Add the lemon juice and oregano. Season to taste.

Pour half the sauce into a 750 ml (26 fl oz/3-cup) ovenproof dish, about 15 cm (6 inches) square. Place the prawns on top. Spoon on the remaining sauce, then crumble the feta over the top. Drizzle with the extra virgin olive oil and sprinkle with freshly cracked black pepper.

Bake for 15 minutes, or until the prawns are just cooked. Garnish with the parsley.

*Garlic Prawns*

# Lobster with Parsley Mayonnaise

☘ SERVES 4
☘ PREPARATION TIME: 25 MINUTES
☘ COOKING TIME: NIL

2 cooked rock lobsters
mixed lettuce leaves, lemon wedges and
    snipped chives, to serve

PARSLEY MAYONNAISE
40 g (1 1/2 oz) parsley sprigs, stalks
    removed, finely chopped
3 teaspoons dijon mustard
1 teaspoon honey
1 tablespoon lemon juice
60 ml (2 fl oz/1/4 cup) pouring
    (whipping) cream
60 g (2 1/4 oz/1/4 cup) mayonnaise

Cut each lobster in half lengthways through the shell. Lift the meat from the tail and body. Crack the legs and prise the meat from them. Remove the cream-coloured vein and soft body matter and discard. Cut the lobster meat into 2 cm (3/4 inch) pieces, cover and refrigerate.

To make the parsley mayonnaise, put the parsley, mustard, honey, lemon juice, cream and mayonnaise in a food processor. Blend until combined, then season. Spoon the mixture into a bowl, cover and refrigerate.

Place a bed of lettuce on each serving plate, top with slices of lobster and spoon parsley mayonnaise over the top.

# Oysters in Potatoes with Cheese Sauce

☘ SERVES 6–8
☘ PREPARATION TIME: 15 MINUTES
☘ COOKING TIME: 25 MINUTES

24 baby new potatoes
vegetable oil, for deep-frying
15 g (1/2 oz) butter
24 fresh oysters
1/2 small onion, finely chopped
1 tablespoon brandy
125 ml (4 fl oz/1/2 cup) pouring
    (whipping) cream
30 g (1 oz/1/4 cup) grated cheddar cheese
2 teaspoons chopped dill

Cook the potatoes in boiling, salted water for 5 minutes, or until tender. Drain and cool. Slice a round from the top of each potato and with a melon baller, scoop a ball from the centre of each. Trim the bases to sit flat.

Fill a saucepan one-third full of the oil and heat to 180°C (350°F), or until a cube of bread dropped into the oil turns brown in 15 seconds. Deep-fry the potatoes until golden, then drain on paper towels.

Melt the butter in a saucepan, add the oysters and toss to seal. Remove from the pan. Add the onion to the pan and fry until soft. Add the brandy and, keeping away from anything flammable, ignite with a match. Allow the flames to die down. Add the cream, bring to the boil, then reduce the heat and simmer until thickened. Remove from the heat, stir in the cheddar and half the dill. Season. Return the oysters to the sauce, then spoon into the potatoes. Grill (broil) until golden brown. Sprinkle with the remaining dill.

*Lobster with Parsley Mayonnaise*

# Rosemary Tuna Kebabs

🌺 SERVES 4
🌺 PREPARATION TIME: 20 MINUTES
🌺 COOKING TIME: 20 MINUTES

3 ripe tomatoes
1 tablespoon olive oil
2–3 small red chillies, seeded and chopped
3–4 garlic cloves, crushed
1 red onion, finely chopped
60 ml (2 fl oz/¼ cup) dry white wine
600 g (1 lb 5 oz) tinned chickpeas,
    drained
3 tablespoons chopped oregano
4 tablespoons chopped flat-leaf (Italian)
    parsley
lemon wedges, to serve

TUNA KEBABS
1 kg (2 lb 4 oz) tuna fillet, cut into cubes
8 rosemary stalks, with leaves
olive oil, for brushing

Cut the tomatoes into halves or quarters and scoop out the seeds. Roughly chop the flesh.

Heat the oil in a large non-stick frying pan. Add the chilli, garlic and onion and stir over medium heat for 5 minutes, or until softened. Add the chopped tomato and the white wine. Cook over low heat for 10 minutes, or until the mixture is soft and pulpy and most of the liquid has evaporated.

Stir in the chickpeas with the oregano and parsley. Season to taste.

Heat a grill (broiler) or barbecue plate. Thread the tuna onto the rosemary stalks, lightly brush with oil, then cook, turning, for 3 minutes. Do not overcook or the tuna will be dry and fall apart. Serve with the chickpeas and lemon wedges.

# Garlic and Ginger Prawns

🌺 SERVES 4

🌺 PREPARATION TIME: 25 MINUTES

🌺 COOKING TIME: 10 MINUTES

1 kg (2 lb 4 oz) large raw prawns (shrimp)

2 tablespoons vegetable oil

3–4 garlic cloves, finely chopped

5 cm (2 inch) piece fresh ginger, cut into
thin matchsticks

2–3 small red chillies, seeded and finely
chopped

6 coriander (cilantro) roots, finely
chopped

8 spring onions (scallions), cut diagonally
into short lengths

½ red capsicum (pepper), thinly sliced

2 tablespoons lemon juice

125 ml (4 fl oz/½ cup) white wine

2 teaspoons grated palm sugar (jaggery)

2 teaspoons fish sauce, or to taste

1 tablespoon coriander (cilantro) leaves,
to garnish

Peel the prawns, leaving the tails intact. Gently cut a slit down the back of each prawn and remove the dark vein from each. Press each prawn out flat.

Heat a wok until very hot, add the oil and swirl to coat the base and side. Stir-fry half of the prawns, garlic, ginger, chilli and coriander root for 1–2 minutes over high heat, or until the prawns have just turned pink, then remove from the wok and set aside. Repeat with the remaining prawns, garlic, ginger, chilli and coriander root. Remove and set aside.

Add the spring onion and capsicum to the wok and cook over high heat for 2–3 minutes. Combine the lemon juice, wine and palm sugar, then add to the wok. Boil until the liquid has reduced by two-thirds.

Return the prawns to the wok and sprinkle with the fish sauce to taste. Toss until the prawns are heated through. Remove from the heat and serve sprinkled with coriander.

# Clams in Chilli Paste

🌸 SERVES 4
🌸 PREPARATION TIME: 15 MINUTES
🌸 COOKING TIME: 12–15 MINUTES

CHILLI PASTE
2 tablespoons vegetable oil
2 spring onions (scallions), sliced
2 garlic cloves, sliced
85 g (3 oz/¼ cup) dried shrimp
6 small fresh red chillies, seeded
2 teaspoons grated palm sugar (jaggery)
2 teaspoons fish sauce
2 teaspoons tamarind purée

1 kg (2 lb 4 oz) fresh clams (vongole)
3 garlic cloves, thinly sliced
3 small red chillies, seeded and sliced
    lengthways
1 tablespoon light soy sauce
250 ml (9 fl oz/1 cup) fish or chicken
    stock
1 handful Thai basil
steamed rice, to serve

To make the chilli paste, heat the oil in a wok over medium heat and fry the spring onion, garlic, dried shrimp and chilli for 3 minutes, or until golden brown. Remove from the wok with a slotted spoon. Reserve the oil in the wok.

Place the shrimp mixture and palm sugar in a mortar and pestle or small food processor and pound or process until well blended. Add the fish sauce, tamarind purée and a pinch of salt and continue to blend to obtain a finely textured paste.

Soak the clams in cold water for 30 minutes. Discard any broken clams or open ones that don't close when tapped on the bench.

Heat the reserved oil in the wok. Add the garlic, chilli, soy sauce and chilli paste. Mix well, then add the stock and bring just to the boil. Add the clams and cook over medium–high heat for 2–3 minutes. Discard any unopened clams. Stir in the basil and serve immediately with steamed rice.

NOTE: Dried shrimp are available from Asian food stores. They are delicious in stir-fries and salads. Store in an airtight container.

# Fried Whitebait

🌸 SERVES 6
🌸 PREPARATION TIME: 10 MINUTES
🌸 COOKING TIME: 10 MINUTES

40 g (1$^1/_2$ oz/$^1/_3$ cup) plain (all-purpose)
   flour
30 g (1 oz/$^1/_4$ cup) cornflour (cornstarch)
2 teaspoons finely chopped flat-leaf
   (Italian) parsley
vegetable oil, for deep-frying
500 g (1 lb 2 oz) whitebait
1 lemon, cut into wedges, to serve

Combine the sifted flours and parsley in a bowl
and season.

Fill a deep, heavy-based frying pan one-third full of oil
and heat to 180°C (350°F), or until a cube of bread
dropped into the oil browns in 15 seconds.

Toss the whitebait in the flour mixture, shake off the
excess flour, and deep-fry in batches for 1$^1/_2$ minutes,
or until pale and crisp. Drain well on crumpled paper
towels. Serve with lemon wedges.

# Lobster Thermidor

🌸 SERVES 2
🌸 PREPARATION TIME: 25 MINUTES
🌸 COOKING TIME: 5–10 MINUTES

1 cooked lobster
80 g (2$^3/_4$ oz) butter
4 spring onions (scallions), finely chopped
2 tablespoons plain (all-purpose) flour
$^1/_2$ teaspoon dry mustard
2 tablespoons white wine or sherry
250 ml (9 fl oz/1 cup) milk
60 ml (2 fl oz/$^1/_4$ cup) pouring (whipping)
   cream
1 tablespoon chopped flat-leaf (Italian)
   parsley
60 g (2$^1/_4$ oz) gruyère cheese, grated

Using a knife, cut the lobster in half lengthways
through the shell. Lift the meat from the tail and body.
Remove the cream-coloured vein and soft body matter
and discard. Cut the meat into 2 cm ($^3/_4$ inch) pieces,
cover and refrigerate. Wash the head and shell halves,
then drain and pat dry.

In a frying pan, heat 60 g (2$^1/_4$ oz) of the butter, add
the spring onion and stir for 2 minutes. Stir in the
flour and mustard and cook for 1 minute, or until
foaming. Add the wine or sherry and the milk and stir
until the mixture thickens. Reduce the heat and
simmer for 1 minute. Stir in the cream, parsley and
lobster meat, then season. Stir over low heat until
heated through. Spoon the mixture into the lobster
shells, sprinkle with the cheese and dot with the
remaining butter. Place under the grill (broiler) for
2 minutes, or until lightly browned.

*Fried Whitebait*

# Barbecued Octopus

⚜ SERVES 6
⚜ PREPARATION TIME: 15 MINUTES
⚜ COOKING TIME: 5 MINUTES

170 ml (5½ fl oz/⅔ cup) olive oil
10 g (¼ oz) chopped oregano
3 tablespoons chopped flat-leaf (Italian)
   parsley
1 tablespoon lemon juice
3 small red chillies, seeded and finely
   chopped
3 garlic cloves, crushed
1 kg (2 lb 4 oz) baby octopus
lime wedges, to serve

To make the marinade, combine the oil, herbs, lemon juice, chilli and garlic in a large bowl and mix well.

Use a small, sharp knife to remove the octopus heads. Grasp the bodies and push the beaks out from the centre with your index finger, then remove and discard. Slit the heads and remove the gut. If the octopus are too large, cut them into smaller portions.

Mix the octopus with the herb marinade. Cover and refrigerate for several hours, or overnight. Drain and reserve the marinade. Cook on a very hot, lightly oiled barbecue or in a very hot frying pan for 3–5 minutes, or until the flesh turns white. Turn frequently and brush generously with the marinade during cooking.

# Grilled Squid

⚜ SERVES 6
⚜ PREPARATION TIME: 10 MINUTES
⚜ COOKING TIME: 10 MINUTES

1 kg (2 lb 4 oz) squid
250 ml (9 fl oz/1 cup) olive oil
2 tablespoons lemon juice
2 garlic cloves, crushed
2 tablespoons chopped oregano
2 tablespoons chopped flat-leaf (Italian)
   parsley, to serve
6 lemon wedges, to serve

To clean the squid, gently pull the tentacles away from the tube (the intestines should come away at the same time). Remove the intestines from the tentacles by cutting under the eyes, then remove the beak if it remains in the centre of the tentacles by using your fingers to push up the centre. Pull away the quill from inside the body and remove. Remove and discard any white membrane. Under cold running water pull away the skin from the hood. Cut the hood into 1 cm (½ inch) rings and place in the bowl with the tentacles. Add the oil, lemon juice, garlic and oregano to the bowl, and toss to coat the squid. Leave to marinate for 30 minutes.

Heat a barbecue or chargrill pan until hot. Drain the squid rings and cook them in batches for 1–2 minutes on each side.

Season the squid rings and sprinkle with the parsley. Serve with lemon wedges.

*Barbecued Octopus*

# Stuffed Prawn Omelettes

MAKES: 8
PREPARATION TIME: 25 MINUTES
COOKING TIME: 15 MINUTES

500 g (1 lb 2 oz) raw prawns (shrimp)
1½ tablespoons vegetable oil
4 eggs, lightly beaten
2 tablespoons fish sauce
8 spring onions (scallions), chopped
6 coriander (cilantro) roots, chopped
2 garlic cloves, chopped
1 small red chilli, seeded and chopped
2 teaspoons lime juice
2 teaspoons grated palm sugar (jaggery)
  or soft brown sugar
3 tablespoons chopped coriander (cilantro)
  leaves
1 small red chilli, sliced, to garnish
coriander (cilantro) sprigs, to garnish
sweet chilli sauce, to serve

Peel the prawns, gently pull out the dark vein from each prawn back, starting from the head end, then chop the prawn meat.

Heat a wok over high heat, add 2 teaspoons of the oil and swirl to coat. Combine the egg with half of the fish sauce. Add 2 tablespoons of the mixture to the wok and swirl to a 16 cm (6¼ inch) round. Cook for 1 minute, then gently lift out. Repeat with the remaining egg mixture to make eight omelettes.

Heat the remaining oil in the wok. Add the prawns, spring onion, coriander root, garlic and chopoped chilli. Stir-fry for 3–4 minutes, or until the prawns are cooked. Stir in the lime juice, palm or brown sugar, coriander leaves and the remaining fish sauce.

Divide the prawn mixture among the omelettes and fold each into a small firm parcel. Cut a slit in the top and garnish with the sliced chilli and the coriander sprigs. Serve with sweet chilli sauce.

# Seafood Quenelles

❁ SERVES 4
❁ PREPARATION TIME: 30 MINUTES
❁ COOKING TIME: 40 MINUTES

QUENELLES

200 g (7 oz) skinless firm white fish fillets
150 g (5½ oz) scallops
150 g (5½ oz) raw prawn (shrimp) meat
1 egg white
1 teaspoon finely grated lemon zest
125 ml (4 fl oz/½ cup) pouring
    (whipping) cream
3 tablespoons finely snipped chives

TOMATO COULIS

1 tablespoon olive oil
1 garlic clove, crushed
425 g (15 oz) tinned crushed tomatoes
170 ml (5½ fl oz/⅔ cup) fish stock or
    water
2 tablespoons pouring (whipping) cream
2 tablespoons snipped chives
1 litre (35 fl oz/4 cups) fish stock

To make the quenelles, pat the fish, scallops and prawn meat dry with paper towels. Roughly mince the fish in a food processor for 30 seconds, then remove. Process the scallops and prawn meat, then return the fish to the processor, add the egg white and lemon zest, and process for about 30 seconds, or until finely minced. With the motor running, slowly pour in the cream until the mixture just thickens — do not overprocess. Stir in the chives, then transfer to a bowl. Cover and refrigerate for at least 3 hours.

Using two wet tablespoons, mould 2 tablespoons of mixture at a time into egg shapes. Place on a baking tray lined with baking paper. Cover and refrigerate for 30 minutes.

To make the tomato coulis, heat the oil in a saucepan, add the garlic and stir over medium heat for about 30 seconds. Add the tomatoes, stock or water, and season. Simmer for 30 minutes, stirring occasionally, until thickened and reduced.

Push the tomato mixture through a fine sieve, discard the pulp and return the liquid to the cleaned pan. Add the cream and chives and reheat gently, stirring.

In a large frying pan, heat the fish stock until just simmering, but be careful not to boil the stock. Gently lower the quenelles into the poaching liquid in batches, then cover the pan, reduce the heat and poach each batch for about 5–6 minutes, or until cooked through. Lift out using a slotted spoon and drain on crumpled paper towels.

Spoon some of the tomato coulis onto each serving plate and top with the seafood quenelles.

# Coconut Prawns with Chilli Dressing

❀ SERVES 4

❀ PREPARATION TIME: 35 MINUTES

❀ COOKING TIME: 30 MINUTES

24 large raw prawns (shrimp)

plain (all-purpose) flour, to coat

1 egg

1 tablespoon milk

60 g (2¼ oz/1 cup) shredded coconut

1 handful coriander (cilantro) leaves,
    chopped

2½ tablespoons vegetable oil

300 g (10½ oz) red Asian shallots,
    chopped

2 garlic cloves, finely chopped

2 teaspoons finely chopped fresh ginger

1 red chilli, seeded and thinly sliced

1 teaspoon ground turmeric

270 ml (9½ fl oz) tinned coconut cream

2 makrut (kaffir lime) leaves, thinly sliced

2 teaspoons lime juice

2 teaspoons grated palm sugar (jaggery)

3 teaspoons fish sauce

vegetable oil, for deep-frying

1 tablespoon chopped coriander (cilantro)
    leaves, extra

Peel the prawns and gently pull out the dark vein from each prawn back, starting from the head end. Holding the prawns by their tails, coat them in flour, then dip them into the combined egg and milk, and then in the combined coconut and coriander. Refrigerate for 30 minutes.

To make the chilli dressing, heat the oil in a saucepan and cook the shallots, garlic, ginger, chilli and turmeric over medium heat for 3–5 minutes, or until fragrant. Add the coconut cream, makrut leaves, lime juice, palm sugar and fish sauce. Bring to the boil, then reduce the heat and simmer for 2–3 minutes, or until thick. Keep warm.

Fill a wok or deep heavy-based saucepan one-third full of oil and heat to 180°C (350°F), or until a cube of bread dropped into the oil browns in 15 seconds. Holding the prawns by their tails, gently lower them into the wok and cook in batches for 3–5 minutes, or until golden. Drain on crumpled paper towel and season with salt.

Add the extra coriander to the chilli dressing and serve with the prawns.

# Stuffed Sardines

🌿 SERVES 4–6

🌿 PREPARATION TIME: 20 MINUTES

🌿 COOKING TIME: 25 MINUTES

1 kg (2 lb 4 oz) butterflied fresh sardines
60 ml (2 fl oz/¼ cup) olive oil
40 g (1½ oz/½ cup) fresh white
    breadcrumbs
30 g (1 oz/¼ cup) sultanas (golden
    raisins)
40 g (1½ oz/¼ cup) pine nuts, toasted
20 g (¾ oz) tinned anchovy fillets,
    drained and mashed
1 tablespoon finely chopped flat-leaf
    (Italian) parsley
2 spring onions (scallions), finely chopped

Preheat the oven to 200°C (400°F/Gas 6). Grease a baking dish. Open out each sardine and place, skin side down, on a chopping board.

Heat half the oil in a frying pan. Add the breadcrumbs and cook over medium heat, stirring until light golden. Drain on paper towels.

Put half the fried breadcrumbs in a bowl and stir in the sultanas, pine nuts, anchovies, parsley and spring onion. Season to taste. Spoon about 2 teaspoons of the mixture into each prepared sardine, then carefully fold up to enclose the stuffing.

Place the stuffed sardines in a single layer in the baking dish. Sprinkle any remaining stuffing over the top of the sardines, along with the cooked breadcrumbs. Drizzle with the remaining olive oil and bake for 15–20 minutes.

# Clams in White Wine

🌸 SERVES 4

🌸 PREPARATION TIME: 10 MINUTES

🌸 COOKING TIME: 20 MINUTES

1 kg (2 lb 4 oz) clams (vongole) (see Note)
2 large tomatoes
2 tablespoons olive oil
1 small onion, finely chopped
2 garlic cloves, crushed
1 tablespoon chopped flat-leaf (Italian)
    parsley
pinch freshly grated nutmeg
80 ml (2½ fl oz/⅓ cup) dry white wine
flat-leaf (Italian) parsley, to garnish

Soak the clams in salted water for 1 hour to release any grit. Rinse under running water and discard any open clams. Score a cross in the base of each tomato. Put in a heatproof bowl and cover with boiling water. Leave for 30 seconds, then transfer to cold water. Drain and peel the skin away from the cross. Cut the tomatoes in half, scoop out the seeds and finely chop.

Heat the oil in a large flameproof casserole dish and cook the onion over low heat for 5 minutes, or until softened. Add the garlic and tomato and cook for 5 minutes. Stir in the chopped parsley and the nutmeg, and season. Add 80 ml (2½ fl oz/⅓ cup) water. Add the clams and cook over low heat until they open. Discard any that don't open. Add the wine and cook over low heat for 3–4 minutes, or until the sauce thickens. Sprinkle parsley on top and serve.

NOTE: You can use mussels instead of clams in this recipe.

# Creamy Baked Scallops

- SERVES 4
- PREPARATION TIME: 20 MINUTES
- COOKING TIME: 10 MINUTES

24 scallops, on the shell
250 ml (9 fl oz/1 cup) fish stock
250 ml (9 fl oz/1 cup) dry white wine
60 g (2¼ oz) butter
4 spring onions (scallions), chopped
1 bacon slice, finely chopped
100 g (3½ oz) button mushrooms, thinly
    sliced
30 g (1 oz/¼ cup) plain (all-purpose)
    flour
185 ml (6 fl oz/¾ cup) pouring
    (whipping) cream
1 teaspoon lemon juice
80 g (2¾ oz/1 cup) fresh breadcrumbs
30 g (1 oz) butter, extra, melted

Slice or pull off any vein, membrane or hard white muscle from the scallops, leaving any roe attached. Remove the scallops from the shells and cut the scallops in half. Rinse and reserve the shells.

Heat the fish stock and white wine in a saucepan and add the scallops. Cover and simmer over medium heat for 2–3 minutes, or until the scallops are opaque and tender. Remove the scallops with a slotted spoon, cover and set aside. Bring the liquid in the pan to the boil and reduce until 375 ml (13 fl oz/1½ cups) remain.

Melt the butter in a saucepan and add the spring onion, bacon and mushrooms. Cook over medium heat for 3 minutes, stirring occasionally, until the spring onion is soft but not brown.

Stir in the flour and cook for 2 minutes. Remove from the heat and gradually stir in the reduced stock. Return to the heat and stir until the mixture boils and thickens. Reduce the heat and simmer for 2 minutes. Stir in the cream and lemon juice and season to taste. Cover, set aside and keep warm.

Combine the breadcrumbs and melted butter in a small bowl. Preheat the grill (broiler) to high.

Divide the scallops among the shells. Spoon the warm sauce over the scallops and sprinkle with the breadcrumb mixture. Place under the grill until the breadcrumbs are golden brown. Serve immediately.

# Prawn Cocktails

🌿 SERVES 4

🌿 PREPARATION TIME: 20 MINUTES

🌿 COOKING TIME: NIL

60 g (2¼ oz/¼ cup) whole-egg
    mayonnaise
2 teaspoons tomato sauce
dash of Tabasco sauce
¼ teaspoon worcestershire sauce
2 teaspoons thick (double/heavy) cream
¼ teaspoon lemon juice
24 cooked large prawns (shrimp)
4 lettuce leaves, shredded
lemon wedges, to serve

Mix the mayonnaise, sauces, cream and juice together in a small bowl.

Peel the prawns, leaving the tails intact on eight of them. Gently pull out the dark vein from the back of each prawn, starting at the head end.

Divide the lettuce among four glasses. Arrange the prawns without the tails in the glasses and drizzle with the sauce. Hang two of the remaining prawns over the edge of each glass and serve with lemon wedges.

# Brandade de Morue

🌿 SERVES 6

🌿 PREPARATION TIME: 25 MINUTES

🌿 COOKING TIME: 45 MINUTES

450 g (1 lb) salt cod (this is the dried
    weight and is about half a cod)
200 g (7 oz) roasting potatoes, cut into
    3 cm (1¼ inch) chunks
150 ml (5 fl oz) olive oil
250 ml (9 fl oz/1 cup) milk
4 garlic cloves, crushed
2 tablespoons lemon juice
olive oil, extra, to drizzle

Put the salt cod in a large bowl, cover with cold water and soak for 24 hours, changing the water frequently. Drain the cod and place in a large saucepan of clean water. Bring to the boil over medium heat, reduce the heat and simmer for 30 minutes. Drain, then cool for 15 minutes.

Meanwhile, cook the potatoes in a saucepan of boiling, salted water for 12–15 minutes, or until tender. Drain and keep warm.

Remove the skin from the fish and break the flesh into large flaky pieces, discarding any bones. Put the flesh in a food processor. Using two separate pans, gently warm the oil in one, and the milk and garlic in another.

Start the food processor and, with the motor running, alternately add small amounts of the milk and oil until you have a thick, paste-like mixture. Add the potato and process this in short bursts until combined. Transfer to a bowl and add the lemon juice, to taste, and freshly ground black pepper. Fluff up the mixture with a fork. Drizzle with the oil before serving. Serve warm or cold.

*Prawn Cocktails*

# Stuffed Crab

🌺 SERVES 4
🌺 PREPARATION TIME: 30 MINUTES
🌺 COOKING TIME: 50 MINUTES

4 live crabs (about 750 g/1 lb 10 oz each)
   (see Note)
55 g (2 oz/¼ cup) salt
80 ml (2½ fl oz/⅓ cup) olive oil
1 onion, finely chopped
1 garlic clove
125 ml (4 fl oz/½ cup) dry white wine
250 ml (9 fl oz/1 cup) tomato passata
   (puréed tomatoes)
¼ teaspoon finely chopped tarragon
2 tablespoons dry breadcrumbs
2 tablespoons chopped flat-leaf (Italian)
   parsley
40 g (1½ oz) butter, chopped into small
   pieces

Put the crabs in the freezer for 1 hour to immobilize them. Bring a large saucepan of water to the boil. Add the salt and the crabs. Return to the boil and simmer, uncovered, for 15 minutes. Remove the crabs from the water and cool for 30 minutes. Extract the meat from the legs. Lift the apron – the small flap on the underside of the crab – and prise off the top hard shell, without destroying the top shell, which is needed for serving. Reserve any liquid in a bowl. Remove the soft internal organs and pull off the grey feathery gills. Take out the meat and chop finely with the leg meat. Scoop out all the brown paste from the shells and mix with the chopped meat.

Heat the oil in a frying pan and cook the onion and garlic for 5–6 minutes, or until softened. Stir in the wine and passata. Simmer for 3–4 minutes, then add any reserved crab liquid. Simmer for 3–4 minutes. Add the crabmeat and tarragon, then season. Simmer for about 5 minutes, until thick. Discard the garlic.

Preheat the oven to 210°C (415°F/Gas 6–7). Rinse out and dry the crab shells. Divide the crab mixture among them, levelling the surface. Combine the breadcrumbs and parsley and sprinkle over the top. Dot with the butter. Bake for 6–8 minutes, until the butter melts and the breadcrumbs brown. Serve hot.

NOTE: The crab traditionally used in this recipe is the centollo or spider crab. Substitute any large-bodied fresh crab, but avoid swimmer or spanner crabs, which do not have enough flesh in them.

# Mussels with Black Beans and Coriander

🌺 SERVES 4

🌺 PREPARATION TIME: 20 MINUTES

🌺 COOKING TIME: 10 MINUTES

1.5 kg (3 lb 5 oz) black mussels

1 tablespoon peanut oil

2 tablespoons black beans, rinsed and
mashed

2 garlic cloves, finely chopped

1 teaspoon finely chopped fresh ginger

2 long red chillies, seeded and finely
chopped

2 teaspoons finely chopped coriander
(cilantro) leaves

1 tablespoon finely chopped coriander
(cilantro) root

60 ml (2 fl oz/¼ cup) Chinese rice wine

2 tablespoons lime juice

2 teaspoons sugar

steamed rice, to serve

Scrub the mussels with a stiff brush and pull out the hairy beards. Discard any broken mussels, or open ones that don't close when tapped on the bench. Rinse well.

Heat a wok until very hot, add the oil and swirl to coat the base and side. Add the black beans, garlic, ginger, chilli, 1 teaspoon coriander leaves and the coriander root, and cook over low heat for 2–3 minutes, or until fragrant. Pour in the rice wine and increase the heat to high. Add half the mussels in a single layer and cover with a tight-fitting lid. Cook for 2–3 minutes, or until the mussels have just opened. Discard any mussels that do not open. Remove from the wok, and repeat with the remaining mussels until all are cooked.

Transfer the mussels to a serving dish, leaving the cooking liquid in the wok. Add the lime juice, sugar and remaining coriander leaves to the wok and cook for 30 seconds. Pour the sauce over the mussels and serve with steamed rice.

# California Rolls

🌼 MAKES 12
🌼 PREPARATION TIME: 25 MINUTES +
🌼 COOKING TIME: 20 MINUTES

220 g (7¾ oz/1 cup) Japanese short-grain
 rice

SUSHI DRESSING
1 tablespoon rice vinegar
2 teaspoons caster (superfine) sugar

1 large egg
1 teaspoon sake
pinch caster (superfine) sugar
1 teaspoon oil
2 sheets nori (dried seaweed), 20 x 18 cm
 (8 x 7 inches), toasted
2 crabsticks, 40 g (1½ oz) each, cut
 into strips
25 g (1 oz) pickled daikon, cut into
 matchsticks
25 g (1 oz) carrot, cut into matchsticks
25 g (1 oz) cucumber, cut into matchsticks
Japanese soy sauce, to serve
wasabi paste, to serve
pickled ginger, to serve

Wash the rice under cold running water until the water runs clear, then drain thoroughly. Leave the rice in the strainer to drain for 1 hour. Put the rice in a saucepan and cover with 300 ml (10½ fl oz) water. Cover the pan and to the boil, then reduce the heat to very low and simmer for 10 minutes. Remove the pan from the heat, remove the lid and put a clean cloth across the top to absorb excess moisture. Set aside for 10 minutes.

To make the sushi dressing, combine the vinegar, sugar and ¼ teaspoon salt in a small bowl.

Spread the rice over the base of a non-metallic dish or bowl, pour the sushi dressing over the top and use a rice paddle or spatula to mix the dressing through the rice, separating the grains as you do so. Fan the rice until it cools to room temperature. Cover with a damp cloth and set it aside, but do not refrigerate.

To make the omelette, gently combine the egg, sake, the pinch of sugar and a pinch of salt. Heat the oil in a small frying pan over medium heat. Add the egg mixture and cook until firm around the edges but still slightly soft in the middle. Roll up the omelette, then tip it out of the pan. Cool, then slice into strips.

Put a nori sheet on a sushi mat, with the nori shiny side down. Top with half the rice, spreading it over the nori, leaving a 2 cm (¾ inch) gap at the edge furthest away from you. Lay half of the fillings on the rice in the following order: omelette, crabstick, daikon, carrot and cucumber. Starting with the end nearest to you, tightly roll up the mat and the nori, making sure you do not tuck the edge of the mat under the roll. Repeat this process with the remaining ingredients.

Using a sharp knife, cut each roll into six slices. After cutting each slice, rinse the knife under cold water to prevent sticking. Serve with soy sauce, wasabi and pickled ginger.

# Seafood Terrine

※ SERVES 8
※ PREPARATION TIME: 1 HOUR
※ COOKING TIME: 40 MINUTES

FIRST LAYER
500 g (1 lb 2 oz) raw prawns (shrimp),
    chilled
2 egg whites, chilled
pinch freshly grated nutmeg
250 ml (9 fl oz/1 cup) pouring
    (whipping) cream, chilled
150 g (5½ oz) baby green beans, trimmed

SECOND LAYER
250 g (9 oz) skinless salmon or ocean
    trout fillet, chopped
2 egg whites, chilled
2 tablespoons snipped chives
250 ml (9 fl oz/1 cup) pouring
    (whipping) cream, chilled

TOMATO COULIS
750 g (1 lb 10 oz) very ripe roma (plum)
    tomatoes
2 tablespoons extra virgin olive oil
1 onion, very finely chopped
2 tablespoons Grand Marnier (optional)
trimmed watercress, to garnish

Preheat the oven to 180°C (350°F/Gas 4). Brush a 1.5 litre (52 fl oz/6-cup) loaf (bar) tin, measuring 12 x 22 cm (4½ x 8½ inches), with oil and line the base with baking paper.

To make the first layer, peel the prawns and gently pull out the dark vein from each prawn back, starting at the head end. Finely chop the prawns in a food processor. Add the egg whites one at a time, processing until smooth. Season. Gradually add the cream. Don't overprocess or it may curdle. Spoon into the prepared loaf tin, cover and refrigerate. Cook the beans in boiling water for 3 minutes, or until just tender, then drain and plunge into cold water. Drain and dry with paper towels. Arrange lengthways over the prawn mixture.

To make the second layer, process the fish in a food processor until finely chopped. Add the egg whites one at a time and process until smooth. Add the chives. Gradually pour in the cream. Do not overprocess or it may curdle. Spread evenly over the beans.

Cover the terrine tightly with foil brushed with oil and put in a baking tray. Pour cold water into the tray to come halfway up the side of the tin. Bake for 35 minutes, or until lightly set in the centre. Cool before removing the foil. Cover with plastic wrap and refrigerate until firm. Serve at room temperature.

Meanwhile, to make the tomato coulis, score a cross in the base of each tomato. Put in a heatproof bowl and cover with boiling water. Leave for 30 seconds, then transfer to cold water, drain and peel away the skin from the cross. Cut the tomatoes in half, scoop out the seeds and chop the flesh. Heat the oil in a saucepan, add the onion and stir for 2–3 minutes, or until tender. Add the tomato and cook over medium heat, stirring often, for 8 minutes, or until reduced and thickened. Stir in the Grand Marnier and cook for 1 minute. Cool, then process in a food processor until smooth. Season and serve with slices of terrine, garnished with watercress.

# Marinated Salmon Strips

❁ SERVES 4

❁ PREPARATION TIME: 15 MINUTES +

❁ COOKING TIME: NIL

2 sashimi-grade salmon fillets, each about 400 g (14 oz), skinned

4 cm (1½ inch) piece fresh ginger, grated

1 garlic clove, finely chopped

3 spring onions (scallions), finely chopped

1 teaspoon sugar

2 tablespoons Japanese soy sauce

125 ml (4 fl oz/½ cup) sake

pickled ginger, to garnish

pickled cucumber, to garnish (available at Asian food stores)

Cut the salmon into thin strips and arrange them in a single layer in a large deep dish.

Put the ginger, garlic, spring onion, sugar, 1 teaspoon salt, soy sauce and sake in a small bowl and stir to combine. Pour the marinade over the salmon, cover and refrigerate for 1 hour.

Arrange the salmon, strip by strip, on a serving plate. Garnish with the pickled ginger and cucumber and serve chilled.

# Prawn Croustade

❁ SERVES 6

❁ PREPARATION TIME: 45 MINUTES

❁ COOKING TIME: 25 MINUTES

½ loaf unsliced white bread, crust removed

125 ml (4 fl oz/½ cup) olive oil

1 garlic clove, crushed

FILLING

500 g (1 lb 2 oz) raw prawns (shrimp)

375 ml (13 fl oz/1½ cups) fish stock

2 slices lemon

50 g (1¾ oz) butter

6 spring onions (scallions), chopped

30 g (1 oz) plain (all-purpose) flour

1 tablespoon lemon juice

½–1 teaspoon chopped dill

60 ml (2 fl oz/¼ cup) pouring (whipping) cream

Preheat the oven to 210°C (415°F/Gas 6–7). Cut the bread into slices 5 cm (2 inches) thick. Cut each slice diagonally to form triangles. Cut another triangle 1 cm (½ inch) inside each piece, then scoop out the centres to create cavities for the filling, leaving a base on each. Heat the oil and garlic in a frying pan, brush all over the bread cases, then bake for 10 minutes, or until golden.

To make the filling, peel the prawns and pull out the dark vein from each prawn back, starting at the head end. Chop the prawns, put in a saucepan and cover with the stock. Add the lemon, simmer for 15 minutes, strain and reserve the liquid and prawns separately. Melt the butter in a saucepan, add the spring onion and stir until soft. Stir in the flour and cook for 2 minutes. Add in the reserved prawn liquid and stir for 5 minutes, or until the sauce thickens. Add the lemon juice, dill, cream and prawns, and stir until heated through. To serve, spoon the filling into the warm bread cases.

*Marinated Salmon Strips*

# Squid with Green Peppercorns

✿ SERVES 4
✿ PREPARATION TIME: 10 MINUTES
✿ COOKING TIME: 5 MINUTES

600 g (1 lb 5 oz) squid tubes, washed and
    dried
2 teaspoons chopped coriander (cilantro)
    root
3 garlic cloves, crushed
80 ml (2½ fl oz/⅓ cup) vegetable oil
25 g (1 oz) Thai green peppercorns on the
    stalk, in brine, or lightly crushed
    fresh peppercorns
2 tablespoons Thai mushroom soy sauce
½ teaspoon grated palm sugar (jaggery)
    or soft brown sugar
1 large handful Thai basil

Cut the squid tubes in half lengthways. Clean and remove the quills. Score a diamond pattern on the inside of the squid. Cut into 4 cm (1½ inch) square pieces.

Put the coriander root, 1 garlic clove and 1 tablespoon of the oil in a food processor and process to form a smooth paste. Mix together the paste and squid pieces, cover and marinate in the fridge for 30 minutes.

Heat a wok over high heat, add the remaining oil and swirl to coat. Add the squid pieces and the remaining garlic and stir-fry for 1 minute. Add the peppercorns and stir-fry for a further 2 minutes, or until the squid is just cooked — it will toughen if overcooked. Add the soy sauce and palm sugar, and stir until the sugar has dissolved. Serve immediately, garnished with Thai basil.

# Asian Oysters

❀ SERVES 4
❀ PREPARATION TIME: 15 MINUTES
❀ COOKING TIME: 5 MINUTES

12 oysters, on the shell
2 garlic cloves, finely chopped
2 x 2 cm (³/₄ x ³/₄ inch) piece fresh ginger,
   cut into thin batons
2 spring onions (scallions), thinly sliced,
   diagonally
60 ml (2 fl oz/¹/₄ cup) Japanese soy sauce
60 ml (2 fl oz/¹/₄ cup) peanut oil
coriander (cilantro) leaves, to garnish

Line a large bamboo steamer with baking paper. Arrange the oysters in a single layer on top.

Put the garlic, ginger and spring onion in a bowl, mix together well, then sprinkle over the oysters. Spoon 1 teaspoon of soy sauce over each oyster. Cover and steam over a wok of simmering water for 2 minutes.

Heat the peanut oil in a small saucepan until smoking and carefully drizzle a little over each oyster. Garnish with the coriander leaves and serve immediately.

# Scallop Ceviche

❀ SERVES 2–4
❀ PREPARATION TIME: 20 MINUTES
❀ COOKING TIME: NIL

16 scallops, on the shell
1 teaspoon finely grated lime zest
2 garlic cloves, chopped
2 red chillies, seeded and chopped
60 ml (2 fl oz/¹/₄ cup) lime juice
1 tablespoon chopped flat-leaf (Italian)
   parsley
1 tablespoon olive oil

Take the scallops off their shells. Rinse and reserve the shells. If the scallops need to be cut off, use a small, sharp knife to slice them free, being careful to leave as little meat on the shell as possible. Slice or pull off any vein, membrane or hard white muscle, leaving any roe attached.

In a non-metallic bowl, mix together the lime zest, garlic, chilli, lime juice, parsley and olive oil, and season. Put the scallops in the dressing and stir to coat. Cover with plastic wrap and refrigerate for 2 hours to 'cook' the scallop meat.

To serve, slide each scallop back onto a half shell and spoon the dressing over. Serve cold.

*Asian Oysters*

# Moules Marinière

🌸 SERVES 4

🌸 PREPARATION TIME: 15 MINUTES

🌸 COOKING TIME: 35 MINUTES

24 black mussels
1 celery stalk, chopped
250 ml (9 fl oz/1 cup) dry white wine
3 onions, chopped
375 ml (13 fl oz/1½ cups) fish stock
4 flat-leaf (Italian) parsley sprigs
1 thyme sprig
1 bay leaf
60 g (2¼ oz) butter
2 garlic cloves, crushed
1 teaspoon plain (all-purpose) flour
dill sprigs, to garnish

Scrub the mussels with a stiff brush and pull out the hairy beards. Discard any broken mussels, or open ones that don't close when tapped on the bench. Rinse well.

Put the mussels, celery, wine and one-third of the onion in a large saucepan and bring rapidly to the boil. Cover and cook, shaking the pan frequently, for 4–5 minutes, discarding any unopened mussels after that time.

Pull off and discard the empty side of each shell. Set aside the mussels in the shells, cover and keep warm.

Strain and reserve the cooking liquid, discarding the vegetables.

In a saucepan, heat the fish stock, parsley, thyme and bay leaf. Bring to the boil, then reduce the heat, cover and simmer for 10 minutes. Remove the herbs.

Melt the butter in a large saucepan, add the garlic and remaining onion and stir over low heat for 5–10 minutes, or until the onion is soft but not brown. Stir in the flour and cook for 1 minute, or until pale and foaming. Remove from the heat and gradually stir in the reserved mussel liquid and fish stock. Return to the heat and stir until the mixture boils and thickens. Reduce the heat and simmer, uncovered, for about 10 minutes.

Divide the reserved mussels among four soup bowls. Ladle the liquid over the mussels and garnish with the dill sprigs. Serve immediately with slices of crusty bread.

# Scallops Provençale

❀ SERVES 4

❀ PREPARATION TIME: 20 MINUTES

❀ COOKING TIME: 30 MINUTES

20 scallops, on the shell
600 g (1 lb 5 oz) tomatoes
60 ml (2 fl oz/¼ cup) olive oil
1 onion, finely chopped
4 French shallots, finely chopped
60 ml (2 fl oz/¼ cup) dry white wine
60 g (2¼ oz) butter
4 garlic cloves, crushed
2 tablespoons finely chopped flat-leaf
    (Italian) parsley
½ teaspoon thyme
2 tablespoons fresh breadcrumbs

Take the scallops off their shells. Rinse and reserve the shells. If the scallops need to be cut off, use a small, sharp knife to slice them free, being careful to leave as little meat on the shell as possible. Slice or pull off any vein, membrane or hard white muscle, leaving any roe attached.

Score a cross in the base of each tomato. Put the tomatoes in a heatproof bowl and cover with boiling water. Leave for 30 seconds, then transfer to cold water. Drain and peel the skin away from the cross. Cut each tomato in half, scoop out the seeds and finely dice the flesh.

Heat 2 tablespoons of the oil in a frying pan over medium heat until hot, add the onion and shallots, then reduce the heat to low and cook slowly for 5 minutes, or until soft. Add the wine and simmer for several minutes until reduced slightly, then add the tomato. Season and cook, stirring occasionally, for 20 minutes, or until thick and pulpy. Preheat the oven to 180°F (350°F/Gas 4).

Heat the butter and remaining oil in a frying pan over high heat until foamy. Cook half the scallops for 1–2 minutes on each side, or until lightly golden. Remove and repeat with the remaining scallops. Set aside.

Add the garlic to the hot scallop pan and stir for 1 minute. Remove from the heat and stir in the parsley, thyme and breadcrumbs.

To serve, warm the shells on a baking tray in the oven. Put a small amount of tomato mixture on each shell, top with a scallop and sprinkle with the breadcrumb and parsley mixture.

# meat and poultry

# Carpaccio

❀ SERVES 8
❀ PREPARATION TIME: 15 MINUTES
❀ COOKING TIME: NIL

400 g (14 oz) beef eye fillet
1 tablespoon extra virgin olive oil
rocket (arugula) leaves, torn, to serve
60 g (2¼ oz) parmesan cheese, shaved,
    to serve
black olives, cut into slivers, to serve

Remove all the visible fat and sinew from the beef, then freeze for 1–2 hours, until firm but not solid. This makes the meat easier to slice thinly.

Cut paper-thin slices of beef with a large, sharp knife. Arrange on a serving platter and allow to return to room temperature.

Just before serving, drizzle with oil, then scatter with rocket, parmesan and olives.

NOTE: The beef can be cut into slices a few hours in advance, covered and refrigerated. Drizzle with oil and garnish with the other ingredients just before serving.

# Quail in Vine Leaves

❀ SERVES 4

❀ PREPARATION TIME: 15 MINUTES

❀ COOKING TIME: 25 MINUTES

12 black grapes, halved
1 tablespoon olive oil
1 garlic clove, crushed
4 large quail
8 fresh or preserved vine leaves
4 prosciutto slices
black grapes, extra, halved, to garnish

Preheat the oven to 180°C (350°F/Gas 4). Toss the grapes with the oil and garlic. Put six grape halves in the cavity of each quail.

If you are using fresh vine leaves, blanch them for 1 minute in boiling water, then remove the central stem. If using preserved vine leaves, wash them under running water to remove any excess preserving liquid.

Wrap each quail in a piece of prosciutto and place each on top of a vine leaf. Place another vine leaf on top of each quail and wrap into parcels, tying with string to secure. Bake on a baking tray for 20–25 minutes, or until juices run clear when tested with a skewer. Serve garnished with the extra grapes.

# Sweet and Sour Liver

❀ SERVES 4

❀ PREPARATION TIME: 10 MINUTES

❀ COOKING TIME: 10 MINUTES

40 g (1¹⁄₂ oz) butter
80 ml (2¹⁄₂ fl oz/¹⁄₃ cup) olive oil
600 g (1 lb 5 oz) calves' livers, cut into
    long thin slices
80 g (2³⁄₄ oz/1 cup) fresh white
    breadcrumbs
1 tablespoon sugar
2 garlic cloves, crushed
60 ml (2 fl oz/¹⁄₄ cup) red wine vinegar
1 tablespoon chopped flat-leaf (Italian)
    parsley

Heat the butter and half the oil in a heavy-based frying pan over medium heat. Coat the liver in the breadcrumbs, pressing them on firmly with your hands. Shake off the excess and place in the pan when the butter begins to foam. Cook on each side for 1 minute, or until the crust is brown and crisp. Remove from the pan and keep warm.

Add the remaining oil to the frying pan and cook the sugar and garlic over low heat until golden. Add the vinegar and cook for 30 seconds, or until almost evaporated. Add the parsley and pour over the liver. Serve hot or at room temperature.

*Quail in Vine Leaves*

# Chicken Ballottine

🌼 SERVES 8
🌼 PREPARATION TIME: 40 MINUTES
🌼 COOKING TIME: 1 HOUR 45 MINUTES

1.6 kg (3 lb 8 oz) chicken
2 red capsicums (peppers)
1 kg (2 lb 4 oz) silverbeet (Swiss chard)
30 g (1 oz) butter
1 onion, finely chopped
1 garlic clove, crushed
50 g (1¾ oz/½ cup) grated parmesan
    cheese
80 g (2¾ oz/1 cup) fresh breadcrumbs
1 tablespoon chopped oregano
200 g (7 oz) ricotta cheese

To bone the chicken, cut through the skin on the centre back with a sharp knife. Separate the flesh from the bone down one side to the breast, being careful not to pierce the skin. Follow along the bones closely with the knife, gradually easing the meat from the thigh, drumstick and wing. Cut through the thigh bone where it meets the drumstick and cut off the wing tip. Repeat on the other side, then lift the rib cage away, leaving the flesh in one piece and the drumsticks still attached to the flesh. Scrape all the meat from the drumstick and wings, discarding the bones. Turn the wing and drumstick flesh inside the chicken and lay the chicken out flat, skin side down. Refrigerate.

Preheat the oven to 180°C (350°F/Gas 4). Cut the capsicums into large flattish pieces, discarding the membranes and seeds. Cook, skin side up, under a hot grill (broiler) until the skin blisters and blackens. Cool in a plastic bag, then peel.

Discard the stalks from the silverbeet and finely shred the leaves. Melt the butter in a large frying pan and cook the onion and garlic over medium heat for 5 minutes, or until soft. Add the silverbeet and stir until wilted and all the moisture has evaporated. Cool. In a food processor, process the silverbeet and onion mixture with the parmesan, breadcrumbs, oregano and half the ricotta. Season with salt and pepper.

Spread the silverbeet mixture over the chicken and lay the pepper pieces over the top. Form the remaining ricotta into a roll and place across the width of the chicken. Fold the sides of the chicken in and over the filling so they overlap slightly. Tuck the ends in neatly. Secure with toothpicks, then tie with string at 3 cm (1¼ inch) intervals.

Grease a piece of foil and place the chicken in the centre. Roll the chicken up in the foil. Bake on a baking tray for 1¼ hours, or until the juices run clear when a skewer is inserted in the centre. Cool, then refrigerate until cold before removing the foil, toothpicks and string. Cut into 1 cm (½ inch) slices to serve.

# Chicken Liver and Grand Marnier Pâté

❀ SERVES 8
❀ PREPARATION TIME: 20 MINUTES
❀ COOKING TIME: 10 MINUTES

750 g (1 lb 10 oz) chicken livers, well
    trimmed
250 ml (9 fl oz/1 cup) milk
200 g (7 oz) butter, softened
4 spring onions (scallions), finely chopped
1 tablespoon Grand Marnier
1 tablespoon frozen orange juice
    concentrate, thawed
1/2 orange, very thinly sliced

JELLIED LAYER
1 tablespoon orange juice concentrate
1 tablespoon Grand Marnier
310 ml (10$^3$/$_4$ fl oz/1$^1$/$_4$ cups) canned
    chicken consommé, undiluted
2$^1$/$_2$ teaspoons powdered gelatine

Put the chicken livers in a bowl, add the milk and stir to combine. Cover and refrigerate for 1 hour. Drain the livers and discard the milk. Rinse in cold water, drain and pat dry with paper towels.

Melt one-third of the butter in a frying pan, add the spring onion and cook for 2–3 minutes, or until tender, but not brown. Add the livers and cook, stirring, over medium heat for 4–5 minutes, or until just cooked. Remove from the heat and cool a little.

Transfer the livers to a food processor and process until very smooth. Chop the remaining butter, add to the processor with the Grand Marnier and orange juice concentrate and process until creamy. Season, to taste, with salt and freshly ground black pepper. Transfer to a 1.25 litre (44 fl oz/5-cup) serving dish, cover the surface with plastic wrap and chill for 1$^1$/$_2$ hours, or until firm.

For the jellied layer, whisk together the orange juice concentrate, Grand Marnier and 125 ml (4 fl oz/ 1/2 cup) of the consommé in a jug. Sprinkle the gelatine over the liquid in an even layer and leave until the gelatine is spongy – do not stir. Heat the remaining consommé in a pan, remove from the heat and add the gelatine mixture. Stir to dissolve the gelatine, then leave to cool and thicken to the consistency of uncooked egg white, but not set.

Press the orange slices lightly into the surface of the pâté and spoon the thickened jelly evenly over the top. Refrigerate until set. Serve at room temperature with toast or crackers.

NOTE: Grand Marnier is a cognac-based liqueur with an orange flavour.

# Teppan Yaki

❀ SERVES 4

❀ PREPARATION TIME: 45 MINUTES

❀ COOKING TIME: 25 MINUTES

350 g (12 oz) scotch fillet, partially
   frozen, thinly sliced
4 small slender eggplants (aubergines)
100 g (3½ oz) fresh shiitake mushrooms
100 g (3½ oz) small green beans, trimmed
6 baby (pattypan) yellow or green squash
1 red or green capsicum (pepper), seeded
   and membrane removed
6 spring onions (scallions)
200 g (7 oz) tinned bamboo shoots,
   drained
60 ml (2 fl oz/¼ cup) vegetable oil

Place the meat slices in a single layer on a large serving platter, season well and set aside. Trim the ends from the eggplants and cut the flesh into long, very thin diagonal slices. Trim any hard stems from the mushrooms. Top and tail the beans. If the beans are longer than about 7 cm (2¾ inches), cut them in half. Quarter, halve or leave the squash whole, depending on the size. Cut the capsicum into thin strips and slice the spring onions into lengths about 7 cm (2¾ inches) long, discarding the tops. Arrange all the vegetables (including the bamboo shoots) in separate bundles on a plate.

When the diners are seated, heat an electric grill or electric frying pan until very hot and then lightly brush it with the oil. Quickly fry about a quarter of the meat, searing on both sides, and then push it over to the edge of the pan. Add about a quarter of the vegetables and quickly stir-fry, adding a little more oil as needed. Serve a small portion of the meat and vegetables to the diners, who dip the food into a sauce of their choice. Repeat the process with the remaining meat and vegetables, cooking in batches as extra helpings are required. Serve with steamed rice.

# Crispy Lamb with Lettuce

❀ SERVES 4
❀ PREPARATION TIME: 15 MINUTES
❀ COOKING TIME: 20 MINUTES

400 g (14 oz) lamb backstraps or loin
   fillets
2 tablespoons light soy sauce
1 tablespoon Chinese rice wine
2 teaspoons fish sauce
½ teaspoon sesame oil
2 garlic cloves, crushed
1 teaspoon finely grated fresh ginger
40 g (1½ oz/⅓ cup) cornflour
   (cornstarch)
vegetable oil, for deep-frying
12 baby cos (romaine) lettuce leaves
plum sauce, to serve
4 spring onions (scallions), thinly sliced,
   to serve

Wrap the lamb in plastic wrap and put it in the freezer for 30 minutes, or until semi-frozen. Remove the plastic wrap and cut the lamb lengthways into three thin slices, then thinly slice across the grain, so that you have julienne strips. Place in a bowl with the soy sauce, rice wine, fish sauce, sesame oil, garlic and ginger. Mix well to coat, then cover and refrigerate for 2 hours.

Sift the cornflour over the lamb and mix well. Spread the lamb out on a tray and return to the refrigerator, uncovered, for 1 hour.

Preheat the oven to 150°C (300°F/Gas 2). Heat the oil in a wok or deep heavy-based saucepan to 180°C (350°F), or until a cube of bread dropped into the oil browns in 15 seconds. Deep-fry the lamb in batches for 5–6 minutes, or until crisp and browned. Lift the lamb out with a slotted spoon and drain on crumpled paper towel. Keep warm in the oven while you cook the remainder.

To serve, cup a lettuce leaf in your hand. With the other hand, drizzle the inside with a little plum sauce, fill with the lamb mixture and sprinkle with the spring onion. Alternatively, arrange the lettuce, lamb, spring onion and plum sauce in separate dishes for your guests to assemble their own 'cups'.

# Meat Dumplings in Yoghurt Sauce

🌸 SERVES 4–6
🌸 PREPARATION TIME: 40 MINUTES
🌸 COOKING TIME: 35 MINUTES

250 g (9 oz/2 cups) plain (all-purpose)
    flour
60 g (2¼ oz) clarified butter, melted,
    for baking (see Note)
40 g (1½ oz) clarified butter, extra,
    to serve
2 garlic cloves, crushed, to serve
1 tablespoon dried mint, to serve

FILLING
20 g (¾ oz) clarified butter
1 small onion, finely chopped
2 tablespoons pine nuts
250 g (9 oz) minced (ground) lamb
pinch ground allspice

YOGHURT SAUCE
750 g (1 lb 10 oz/3 cups) plain yoghurt
2 teaspoons cornflour (cornstarch)
1 egg white, lightly beaten

To make the dough, sift the flour and 1 teaspoon salt into a bowl and add 185 ml (6 fl oz/¾ cup) water a little at a time and combine until the mixture comes together in a ball. Cover and allow to rest for 30 minutes.

To make the filling, melt the clarified butter in a deep heavy-based frying pan and cook the onion over medium heat for 5 minutes, or until soft. Add the pine nuts and allow them to brown, stirring constantly. Increase the heat to high and add the lamb and allspice, stirring until the meat changes colour. Season and cool.

Preheat the oven to 180°C (350°F/Gas 4). Lightly grease two baking trays. Roll out the dough on a floured board, to about 5 mm (¼ inch) thick and cut into rounds using a 5 cm (2 inch) cutter. Put a teaspoon of filling in the centre of each round and fold the pastry over into a crescent. Press the edges together firmly and then wrap the crescent around one finger and press the two ends together to make a hat shape. Place on the baking trays and brush lightly with the clarified butter. Bake for 10 minutes, or until lightly browned.

To make the sauce, put the yoghurt in a large, heavy-based saucepan and stir until smooth. Combine the cornflour with 375 ml (13 fl oz/1½ cups) water, stir until smooth, then add to the yoghurt with the egg white and 2 teaspoons salt. Cook over medium heat, stirring until the mixture thickens. Add the dumplings to the pan, stir gently, then cook, uncovered, over low heat for 10 minutes, stirring occasionally.

Just before serving, melt the extra clarified butter in a small frying pan and pan-fry the garlic gently for a few seconds. Stir in the mint and remove from the heat. Pour over the dumplings and serve with rice.

NOTE: To clarify butter, heat butter over low heat until liquid. Leave until the white milk solids settle to the bottom. Use a spoon to skim off any foam, then strain off the golden liquid, leaving the white solids behind. Discard the solids.

# Duck Breast with Wild Rice

🌿 SERVES 4

🌿 PREPARATION TIME: 15 MINUTES

🌿 COOKING TIME: 1 HOUR

DRESSING
80 ml (2½ fl oz/⅓ cup) olive oil
1 teaspoon grated orange zest
2 tablespoons orange juice
2 teaspoons walnut oil
1 tablespoon chopped preserved ginger

95 g (3½ oz/½ cup) wild rice
2 teaspoons vegetable oil
50 g (1¾ oz/½ cup) pecans, roughly
    chopped
½ teaspoon ground cinnamon
65 g (2½ oz/⅓ cup) long-grain white
    rice
2 tablespoons finely chopped flat-leaf
    (Italian) parsley
4 spring onions (scallions), thinly sliced
2 duck breasts
zest of 1 orange

To make the dressing, thoroughly mix the ingredients together and season. Set aside.

Put the wild rice in a saucepan with about 300 ml (10½ fl oz) water. Bring to the boil, reduce heat to low and cook, covered, for 30 minutes, or until tender. Drain away any excess water.

Meanwhile, heat the oil in a large frying pan. Add the pecans and cook, stirring, until golden. Add the cinnamon and a pinch of salt, and cook for 1 minute.

Bring a large saucepan of water to the boil. Add the white rice and cook, stirring occasionally, for 12 minutes, or until tender. Drain and mix with the wild rice and pecans in a large, shallow bowl. Add the parsley and spring onion. Add half the dressing and toss well.

Put the duck, skin side down, in a cold frying pan, then heat the pan over high heat. Cook for 5 minutes, or until crisp, then turn over and cook for another 5 minutes. Tip out any excess fat and add the remaining dressing and the orange zest, and cook until bubbling. Transfer the duck to a serving dish and slice, diagonally. Serve with the rice, drizzled with any juices.

# Chicken, Veal and Mushroom Loaf

🌸 SERVES 6
🌸 PREPARATION TIME: 20 MINUTES
🌸 COOKING TIME: 1 HOUR

100 g (3½ oz) pappardelle
20 g (¾ oz/¼ cup) fresh breadcrumbs
1 tablespoon dry white wine
375 g (13 oz) minced (ground) chicken
375 g (13 oz) minced (ground) veal
2 garlic cloves, crushed
100 g (3½ oz) button mushrooms, finely
   chopped
2 eggs, beaten
pinch freshly grated nutmeg
pinch cayenne pepper
60 g (2¼ oz/¼ cup) sour cream
4 spring onions (scallions), finely chopped
2 tablespoons chopped flat-leaf (Italian)
   parsley

Grease a 1.5 litre (52 fl oz/6-cup) loaf tin. Cook the pappardelle in a large saucepan of rapidly boiling salted water until *al dente*. Drain.

Preheat the oven to 200°C (400°F/Gas 6). Soak the breadcrumbs in the wine. Mix the crumbs in a bowl with the chicken, veal, garlic, mushrooms, eggs, nutmeg, cayenne pepper, then season to taste. Mix in the sour cream, spring onion and parsley.

Place half the mince mixture into the prepared tin with your hands. Form a deep trough along the entire length. Fill the trough with the pappardelle. Press the remaining mince mixture over the top. Bake for 50–60 minutes, draining the excess fat and juice from the tin twice during cooking. Cool slightly, then slice.

NOTE: Mushrooms can be chopped in a food processor. Don't prepare too far in advance or they will discolour and darken the loaf.

# Circassian Chicken

🌼 SERVES 6

🌼 PREPARATION TIME: 25 MINUTES

🌼 COOKING TIME: 1 HOUR

2 teaspoons paprika

1/4 teaspoon cayenne pepper

1 tablespoon walnut oil

4 chicken breasts, on the bone

4 chicken wings

1 large onion, chopped

2 celery stalks, roughly chopped

1 carrot, chopped

1 bay leaf

4 sprigs flat-leaf (Italian) parsley

1 sprig thyme

6 peppercorns

1 teaspoon coriander seeds

250 g (9 oz/2 1/2 cups) walnuts, toasted
    (see Note)

2 slices white bread, crusts removed

4 garlic cloves, crushed

1 tablespoon paprika, extra

salad leaves, to serve

Put the paprika and cayenne pepper in a small dry frying pan and heat over low heat for about 2 minutes, or until aromatic. Add the walnut oil to the pan and set aside until ready to use.

Put the chicken pieces in a large saucepan with the onion, celery, carrot, bay leaf, parsley, thyme, peppercorns and coriander seeds. Add about 1 litre (35 fl oz/4 cups) water and bring to the boil. Reduce the heat to low and simmer for 15–20 minutes, or until the chicken is tender. Remove from the heat and allow to cool in the stock. Remove the chicken pieces and return the stock to the heat. Simmer for 20–25 minutes, or until reduced by half. Strain, skim off the fat and reserve the stock. Remove the chicken skin and shred the flesh into bite-sized pieces. Season well and ladle some stock over the chicken to keep it moist. Set aside.

Reserve a few of the walnuts to use as garnish and blend the rest in a food processor to form a rough paste. Combine the bread with 125 ml (4 fl oz/1/2 cup) of the reserved stock, add to the food processor and mix in short bursts for several seconds. Add the garlic and extra paprika, and season. Process until smooth. Gradually add 250 ml (9 fl oz/1 cup) of warm chicken stock until the mixture is of a smooth pourable consistency, adding a little more stock if necessary.

Mix half the sauce with the chicken and place on a serving platter. Pour the rest over to cover, then sprinkle with the spiced walnut mixture and the remaining walnuts. Serve at room temperature on a bed of salad leaves.

NOTE: Californian walnuts are best for this recipe as they are much less bitter than other types of walnut.

# San Choy Bau with Noodles

❋ SERVES 6

❋ PREPARATION TIME: 20 MINUTES

❋ COOKING TIME: 15 MINUTES

500 g (1 lb 2 oz) raw prawns (shrimp)
vegetable oil, for deep-frying
100 g (3½ oz) dried rice vermicelli (see
    Notes)
60 ml (2 fl oz/¼ cup) chicken stock
2 tablespoons Chinese rice wine
2 tablespoons soy sauce
2 tablespoons hoisin sauce
1 tablespoon brown bean sauce
½ teaspoon sugar
60 ml (2 fl oz/¼ cup) peanut oil
1 garlic clove, crushed
1 tablespoon finely chopped fresh ginger
3 spring onions (scallions), thinly sliced
    and green ends reserved, to garnish
150 g (5½ oz) minced (ground) pork (see
    Notes)
12 iceberg lettuce leaves, trimmed into
    neat cups

Peel the prawns and gently pull out the dark vein from each prawn back, starting at the head end. Roughly chop.

Fill a deep heavy-based saucepan or deep-fryer one-third full of oil and heat to 170°C (325°F), or until a cube of bread dropped into the oil browns in 20 seconds. Add the vermicelli to the oil in batches and deep-fry until puffed up but not browned – this will only take a few seconds, so watch it carefully. Remove with a slotted spoon and drain well on crumpled paper towels.

To make the stir-fry sauce, put the stock, rice wine, soy sauce, hoisin sauce, brown bean sauce, sugar and ½ teaspoon salt in a small bowl and stir together until well combined.

Heat the peanut oil in a wok over high heat and swirl to coat. Add the garlic, ginger and spring onion and stir-fry for 1 minute, being careful not to burn the garlic. Add the pork to the wok, breaking up the lumps with the back of a wooden spoon, then cook for 4 minutes. Add the prawn meat and stir-fry for 2 minutes, or until it begins to change colour. Add the stir-fry sauce and stir until combined. Cook over high heat for 2 minutes, or until the mixture thickens slightly.

Divide the noodles among the lettuce cups, spoon the pork and prawn mixture over the noodles and garnish with the reserved spring onion. Serve at once.

NOTES: Have everything you need ready before you start deep-frying – a slotted spoon for removing the noodles and a tray lined with crumpled paper towels. Remember to deep-fry the noodles in small batches as they will dramatically increase in volume when cooked.
    When deep-frying the vermicelli, take care not to allow the oil to become too hot or the noodles will expand and brown very quickly. Make sure the pork mince is not too lean or the mixture will be dry.

# Larb

❀ SERVES 4–6
❀ PREPARATION TIME: 20 MINUTES
❀ COOKING TIME: 10 MINUTES

1 tablespoon vegetable oil
2 lemon grass stems, white part only,
    thinly sliced
2 green chillies, finely chopped
500 g (1 lb 2 oz) lean minced (ground)
    pork or beef
60 ml (2 fl oz/¼ cup) lime juice
2 teaspoons finely grated lime zest
2–6 teaspoons chilli sauce
lettuce leaves, to serve
3 tablespoons chopped coriander (cilantro)
    leaves
2 tablespoons chopped mint
1 small red onion, thinly sliced
50 g (1¾ oz/⅓ cup) unsalted roasted
    peanuts, chopped
25 g (1 oz/¼ cup) crisp-fried garlic

Heat the oil in a wok and stir-fry the lemon grass, chilli and pork or beef over high heat for 6 minutes, or until the meat is cooked, breaking up any lumps. Transfer to a bowl and allow to cool. Add the lime juice, zest and chilli sauce and mix well.

Arrange the lettuce leaves on a serving plate. Stir most of the coriander, mint, onion, peanuts and garlic through the meat mixture, spoon over the lettuce and sprinkle the rest of the coriander, mint, onion, peanuts and garlic over the top.

# Savoury Egg Custard

200 g (7 oz) boneless, skinless chicken breasts, cut into bite-sized pieces
2 teaspoons sake
2 teaspoons Japanese soy sauce
2 leeks, white part only, sliced into matchsticks
1 small carrot, sliced into matchsticks
200 g (7 oz) English spinach, chopped

CUSTARD
1 litre (35 fl oz/4 cups) boiling water
80 g (2¾ oz/½ cup) dashi granules
2 tablespoons Japanese soy sauce
6 eggs

Divide the chicken pieces among six heatproof bowls. Combine the sake and soy sauce and pour over the chicken. Divide the leek, carrot and spinach among the bowls.

To make the custard, combine the boiling water and dashi granules in a heatproof bowl and stir to dissolve. Cool completely. Combine the dashi, soy sauce and eggs, and strain equal amounts into the bowls.

Fill a wok with 500 ml (17 fl oz/2 cups) water and bring to the boil. Cover the bowls with foil, place them in a steamer, then sit the steamer in the wok. Cover and cook over high heat for 20–30 minutes. Test the custard by inserting a fine skewer into the centre — it is cooked when the skewer comes out with no moisture clinging to it. Serve immediately.

# Snails with Garlic and Herb Butter

🌿 SERVES 6
🌿 PREPARATION TIME: 15 MINUTES
🌿 COOKING TIME: 5 MINUTES

400 g (14 oz) tinned snails
125 g (4½ oz) butter, softened
4 garlic cloves, crushed
2 tablespoons chopped flat-leaf (Italian)
    parsley
2 teaspoons snipped chives
36 snail shells (available from speciality
    food stores), or use ovenproof ramekins
    or dariole moulds
20 g (¾ oz/¼ cup) fresh white
    breadcrumbs

Preheat the oven to 200°C (400°F/Gas 6). Rinse the snails under cold water. Drain well and set aside. In a small bowl, combine the butter, garlic, parsley and chives until smooth. Season. Put a small amount of the butter and a snail in each shell. Seal the shells with the remaining butter and sprinkle with the breadcrumbs.

Place the snails on a baking tray with the open end of the snail facing up so that the butter will not run out of the shell. Bake for 5–6 minutes, or until the butter is bubbling and the breadcrumbs are lightly browned. Serve with crusty baguette.

# Cabbage Rolls

❀ MAKES 12 LARGE ROLLS
❀ PREPARATION TIME: 30 MINUTES
❀ COOKING TIME: 1 HOUR 35 MINUTES

1 tablespoon olive oil
1 onion, finely chopped
large pinch ground allspice
1 teaspoon ground cumin
large pinch freshly grated nutmeg
2 bay leaves
1 large head cabbage
500 g (1 lb 2 oz) minced (ground) lamb
220 g (7¾ oz/1 cup) short-grain white rice
4 garlic cloves, crushed
50 g (1¾ oz/⅓ cup) pine nuts, toasted
2 tablespoons chopped mint
2 tablespoons chopped flat-leaf (Italian)
    parsley
1 tablespoon currants, chopped
250 ml (9 fl oz/1 cup) olive oil, extra
80 ml (2½ fl oz/⅓ cup) lemon juice
extra virgin olive oil, to drizzle
lemon wedges, to serve

Heat the oil in a saucepan, add the onion and cook over medium heat for 10 minutes, or until golden. Add the allspice, cumin and nutmeg and cook for 2 minutes, or until fragrant. Remove from the pan.

Bring a very large saucepan of water to the boil and add the bay leaves. Cut the tough outer leaves and about 5 cm (2 inches) of the core from the cabbage, then carefully add the cabbage to the boiling water. Cook it for 5 minutes, then carefully loosen a whole leaf with tongs and remove. Continue to cook and remove the leaves until you reach the core. Drain, reserving the cooking liquid and set aside to cool.

Take 12 leaves of equal size and cut a small 'V' from the core end of each to remove the thickest part. Trim the firm central veins so the leaf is as flat as possible. Use three-quarters of the remaining leaves to line the base of a very large saucepan.

Combine the lamb, onion mixture, rice, garlic, pine nuts, mint, parsley and currants in a bowl and season well. With the core end of the leaf closest to you, form 2 tablespoons of the mixture into an oval and place in the centre of the leaf. Roll up, tucking in the sides. Repeat with the remaining 11 leaves and filling. Place tightly, in a single layer, in the lined saucepan, seam side down.

Combine 625 ml (21½ fl oz/2½ cups) of the reserved cooking liquid with the extra olive oil, lemon juice and 1 teaspoon salt and pour over the rolls (the liquid should just come to the top of the rolls). Lay the remaining cabbage leaves over the top. Cover and bring to the boil over high heat, then reduce the heat and simmer for 1¼ hours, or until the mince and rice are cooked. Carefully remove from the pan with a slotted spoon, then drizzle with the extra virgin olive oil. Serve with the lemon wedges.

# Layered Lamb and Burghul

🌢 SERVES 4–6
🌢 PREPARATION TIME: 30 MINUTES
🌢 COOKING TIME: 55 MINUTES

350 g (12 oz/2 cups) burghul (bulgur)
400 g (14 oz) minced (ground) lamb
1 large onion, finely chopped
1 tablespoon ground cumin
1 teaspoon ground allspice
plain yoghurt, to serve

FILLING
1 tablespoon olive oil, plus extra for
   brushing
1 onion, finely chopped
1 teaspoon ground cinnamon
1 tablespoon ground cumin
500 g (1 lb 2 oz) minced (ground) lamb
85 g (3 oz/²⁄₃ cup) raisins
100 g (3¹⁄₂ oz) pine nuts, toasted
olive oil, for brushing

Soak the burghul in cold water for 30 minutes, then drain and squeeze out excess water. Put the lamb, onion, cumin, allspice and some salt and pepper in a food processor, and process until combined. Add the burghul and process to a paste. Refrigerate until needed. Preheat the oven to 180°C (350°F/Gas 4). Lightly grease a 20 x 30 cm (8 x 12 inch) baking dish.

To make the filling, heat the oil in a large frying pan over medium heat and cook the onion for 5 minutes, or until softened. Add the cinnamon and cumin and stir for 1 minute, or until fragrant. Add the lamb, stirring to break up any lumps, and cook for 5 minutes, or until the meat is brown. Stir in the raisins and pine nuts and season, to taste.

Press half the burghul mixture into the base of the baking dish, smoothing the surface with wet hands. Spread the filling over the top, then cover with the remaining burghul, again smoothing the top.

Score a diamond pattern in the top of the mixture with a knife and brush with olive oil. Bake for 40 minutes, or until the top is brown. Cool for 10 minutes before cutting into diamond shapes. Serve with yoghurt.

# Vietnamese Crepes with Pork, Prawns and Noodles

⚜ SERVES 6

⚜ PREPARATION TIME: 45 MINUTES

⚜ COOKING TIME: 35 MINUTES

290 g (10¼ oz/1⅔ cups) rice flour
1 teaspoon baking powder
1½ teaspoons sugar
½ teaspoon ground turmeric
250 ml (9 fl oz/1 cup) coconut milk
3 teaspoons peanut oil
lime wedges, to serve

DIPPING SAUCE
2 tablespoons lime juice
1 tablespoon fish sauce
1 tablespoon caster (superfine) sugar
1 small red chilli, finely chopped

SALAD
1 carrot, roughly grated
120 g (4¼ oz) iceberg lettuce, shredded
1 Lebanese (short) cucumber, cut into thin
   batons
100 g (3½ oz) bean sprouts, trimmed
2 large handfuls mint
2 large handfuls coriander (cilantro)
   leaves

FILLING
250 g (9 oz) raw prawns (shrimp)
1 small red capsicum (pepper)
80 g (2¾ oz) button mushrooms
4 spring onions (scallions)
80 g (2¾ oz) dried rice vermicelli
1 tablespoon peanut oil
1 large onion, thinly sliced
6 garlic cloves, crushed
200 g (7 oz) lean minced (ground) pork
1 tablespoon light soy sauce
¼ teaspoon ground white pepper

To make the crepe batter, blend the rice flour, baking powder, sugar, turmeric, coconut milk, ½ teaspoon salt and 250 ml (9 fl oz/1 cup) water in a blender to a smooth batter. Cover and leave in a warm place for 2–4 hours.

Mix together all the dipping sauce ingredients in a small bowl.

Toss all the salad ingredients together in a large bowl.

To make the filling, peel the prawns, gently pull out the dark vein from each prawn back, starting at the head end, then chop the prawn meat. Remove the seeds and membrane from the capsicum. Thinly slice the capsicum, mushrooms and spring onions. Break the vermicelli into pieces and soak in boiling water for 6–7 minutes, or until soft. Drain. Heat a wok over high heat, add the peanut oil and swirl to coat. Add the onion and cook for 2 minutes, then add the garlic, cooking for a further 30 seconds. Add the pork and cook for 2 minutes, or until browned. Stir in the prawns, capsicum and mushrooms and cook until the prawns change colour. Stir in the noodles, soy sauce, white pepper and spring onion. Remove from heat.

To make the crepes, whisk the batter until smooth. Heat ½ teaspoon of the oil in a 30 cm (12 inch) non-stick frying pan. Pour 80 ml (2½ fl oz/⅓ cup) of the batter into the centre of the pan, and swirl to spread to the edges. Cook over medium heat for | 1–2 minutes, or until golden and crispy. Turn and repeat on the other side. Repeat with the remaining oil and batter to make six crepes in total.

To assemble, place a portion of the filling on half a crepe, folding the other half on top. Repeat with the remaining crepes and filling. Serve with the dipping sauce, salad and lime wedges.

# Peking Duck with Mandarin Pancakes

🌼 SERVES 6

🌼 PREPARATION TIME: 1 HOUR

🌼 COOKING TIME: 1 HOUR 15 MINUTES

1.7 kg (3 lb 12 oz) duck, washed
3 litres (104 fl oz/12 cups) boiling water
1 tablespoon honey
12 spring onions (scallions)
1 Lebanese (short) cucumber, seeded and
    cut into batons
2 tablespoons hoisin sauce

MANDARIN PANCAKES
310 g (11 oz/2½ cups) plain (all-
    purpose) flour
2 teaspoons caster (superfine) sugar
250 ml (9 fl oz/1 cup) boiling water
1 tablespoon sesame oil

Remove the neck and any large pieces of fat from inside the duck carcass. Hold the duck over the sink and very carefully and slowly pour the boiling water over it, rotating the duck. Put the duck on a rack in an ovenproof dish. Mix the honey with 125 ml (4 fl oz/½ cup) hot water and brush two coats of this glaze all over the duck. Dry in a cool, airy place for about 4 hours.

Preheat the oven to 210°C (415°F/Gas 6–7). Cut an 8 cm (3¼ inch) section from the white end of each spring onion. Make fine parallel cuts from the top of the section towards the white end. Put the spring onion pieces in iced water. Roast the duck for 30 minutes, then turn it over without tearing the skin and roast it for 30 minutes. Remove the duck from the oven and leave for a minute or two, then place it on a warm dish.

Meanwhile, to make the pancakes, put the flour and sugar in a bowl and pour in the boiling water. Stir the mixture a few times and leave until lukewarm. Knead the mixture, on a floured surface, into a smooth dough. Cover and set aside for 30 minutes. Take two level tablespoons of dough and roll each one into a ball. Roll out to circles 8 cm (3¼ inches) in diameter. Brush one of the circles with sesame oil and place the other circle on top. Re-roll to make a thin pancake about 15 cm (6 inches) in diameter. Repeat with the remaining dough and oil to make about 10 'double' pancakes.

Heat a frying pan and cook the pancakes one at a time. When small bubbles appear on the surface, turn the pancake over and cook the second side, pressing the surface with a tea towel. The pancake should puff up when done. Transfer the pancake to a plate. When cool enough to handle, peel the two halves of the double pancake apart. Stack them on a plate and cover.

To serve, thinly slice the duck. Place the pancakes and duck on separate plates. Arrange the cucumber sticks and spring onion brushes on another plate. Put the hoisin sauce in a small dish. Spread a little sauce on a pancake, adds some cucumber, a spring onion brush and a piece of duck. Fold over into a neat envelope.

# pasta, gnocchi and rice

# Spaghetti Carbonara

❀ SERVES 6
❀ PREPARATION TIME: 10 MINUTES
❀ COOKING TIME: 20 MINUTES

500 g (1 lb 2 oz) spaghetti
8 bacon slices
4 eggs
50 g (1¾ oz/½ cup) freshly grated
    parmesan cheese
310 ml (10¾ fl oz/1¼ cups) pouring
    (whipping) cream
snipped chives, to garnish

Cook the spaghetti in a large saucepan of rapidly boiling salted water until *al dente*. Drain and return to the pan.

While the pasta is cooking, discard the bacon rind and cut the bacon into thin strips. Cook in a heavy-based frying pan over medium heat until crisp. Remove and drain on paper towels.

Beat the eggs, parmesan and cream in a bowl until well combined. Add the bacon and pour the sauce over the warm pasta. Toss gently until the pasta is well coated.

Return the pan to the heat and cook over low heat for 1 minute, or until slightly thickened. Season with freshly ground black pepper and serve garnished with snipped chives.

# Fettucine Alfredo

❀ SERVES 6
❀ PREPARATION TIME: 10 MINUTES
❀ COOKING TIME: 15 MINUTES

500 g (1 lb 2 oz) fettucine or tagliatelle
90 g (3¼ oz) butter
150 g (5½ oz/1½ cups) freshly grated
    parmesan cheese
310 ml (10¾ fl oz/1¼ cups) pouring
    (whipping) cream
3 tablespoons chopped flat-leaf (Italian)
    parsley

Cook the pasta in a large saucepan of rapidly boiling salted water until *al dente*. Drain and return to the pan.

Meanwhile, melt the butter in a saucepan over low heat. Add the parmesan and cream and bring to the boil, stirring constantly. Reduce the heat and simmer for 10 minutes, or until the sauce has thickened slightly. Add the parsley, season to taste, and stir well to combine. Add the sauce to the warm pasta and toss well to combine.

*Spaghetti Carbonara*

# Lemon, Herb and Fish Risotto

☘ SERVES 4–6

☘ PREPARATION TIME: 20 MINUTES

☘ COOKING TIME: 30 MINUTES

60 g (2¼ oz) butter
400 g (14 oz) skinless firm white fish
    fillets (such as coley, cod, blue-eye,
    ling), cut into 3 cm (1¼ inch) cubes
1.25 litres (44 fl oz/5 cups) fish stock
1 onion, finely chopped
1 garlic clove, crushed
1 teaspoon ground turmeric
330 g (11¾ oz/1½ cups) risotto rice
2 tablespoons lemon juice
1 tablespoon chopped flat-leaf (Italian)
    parsley
1 tablespoon snipped chives
1 tablespoon chopped dill

Melt half the butter in a frying pan. Add the fish in batches and fry over medium–high heat for 3 minutes, or until the fish is just cooked through. Remove from the pan and set aside.

Pour the fish stock into a saucepan, bring to the boil, cover and keep at simmering point.

To the first pan, add the remaining butter, onion and garlic and cook over medium heat for 3 minutes, or until the onion is tender. Add the turmeric and stir for 1 minute. Add the rice and stir to coat, then add 125 ml (4 fl oz/½ cup) of the fish stock and cook, stirring constantly, over low heat until all the stock has been absorbed. Continue adding 125 ml (4 fl oz/½ cup) of stock at a time until all the stock has been added and the rice is translucent, tender and creamy.

Stir in the lemon juice, parsley, chives and dill. Add the fish and stir gently. Serve garnished with slices of lemon or lime and herb sprigs.

NOTE: The rice must absorb the stock between each addition — the whole process will take about 20 minutes. If you don't have time to make your own stock, you can buy fresh or frozen fish stock from delicatessens, some seafood outlets and most supermarkets.

# Spaghetti with Sardines, Fennel and Tomato

❀ SERVES 4–6

❀ PREPARATION TIME: 30 MINUTES

❀ COOKING TIME: 45 MINUTES

3 roma (plum) tomatoes

80 ml (2½ fl oz/⅓ cup) olive oil

3 garlic cloves, crushed

80 g (2¾ oz/1 cup) fresh white
    breadcrumbs

1 red onion, thinly sliced

1 fennel bulb, quartered and thinly sliced

40 g (1½ oz/⅓ cup) raisins

40 g (1½ oz/¼ cup) pine nuts, toasted

4 anchovy fillets, chopped

125 ml (4 fl oz/½ cup) dry white wine

1 tablespoon tomato paste (concentrated
    purée)

4 tablespoons finely chopped flat-leaf
    (Italian) parsley

350 g (12 oz) butterflied sardine fillets

500 g (1 lb 2 oz) spaghetti

Score a cross in the base of each tomato. Place the tomatoes in a bowl of boiling water for 10 seconds, then plunge into cold water. Drain and peel the skin away from the cross. Cut the tomatoes in half and scoop out the seeds. Roughly chop the tomato flesh.

Heat 1 tablespoon of the oil in a large frying pan over medium heat. Add 1 garlic clove and the breadcrumbs and stir for about 5 minutes, until golden and crisp. Transfer to a plate.

Heat the remaining oil in the same pan and cook the onion, fennel and the remaining garlic for 8 minutes, or until soft. Add the tomato, raisins, pine nuts and anchovies and cook for a further 3 minutes. Add the wine, tomato paste and 125 ml (4 fl oz/½ cup) water. Simmer for 10 minutes, or until the mixture thickens slightly. Stir in the parsley and set aside.

Pat the sardines dry with paper towels. Cook the sardines in batches in a lightly greased frying pan over medium heat for 1 minute, or until cooked through. Take care not to overcook or they will break up. Set aside.

Cook the pasta in a large saucepan of rapidly boiling salted water until *al dente*. Drain and return to the pan.

Stir the sauce through the pasta until the pasta is well coated and the sauce evenly distributed. Add the sardines and half the breadcrumbs and toss gently. Sprinkle the remaining breadcrumbs over the top and serve immediately.

# Parsnip Gnocchi

🌺 SERVES 4
🌺 PREPARATION TIME: 45 MINUTES
🌺 COOKING TIME: 45 MINUTES

500 g (1 lb 2 oz) parsnip
185 g (6½ oz/1½ cups) plain (all-
purpose) flour
50 g (1¾ oz/½ cup) freshly grated
parmesan cheese

GARLIC HERB BUTTER
100 g (3½ oz) butter
2 garlic cloves, crushed
3 tablespoons chopped lemon thyme
1 tablespoon finely grated lime zest

Cut the parsnip into large pieces. Cook in a large saucepan of boiling water for 30 minutes, or until very tender. Drain thoroughly and leave to cool slightly.

Mash the parsnip in a bowl until smooth. Sift the flour into the bowl and add half the parmesan. Season and mix to form a soft dough.

Divide the dough in half. Using floured hands, roll each half of the dough out on a lightly floured surface into a sausage shape 2 cm (¾ inch) wide. Cut each sausage into short pieces, shape each piece into an oval and press the top gently with floured fork prongs.

Lower batches of the gnocchi into a large saucepan of boiling salted water. Cook for about 2 minutes, or until the gnocchi rise to the surface. Use a slotted spoon to transfer to serving plates.

To make the garlic herb butter, combine all the ingredients in a small saucepan and cook over medium heat for 3 minutes, or until the butter is nutty brown.

To serve, drizzle the garlic herb butter over the gnocchi and sprinkle with the remaining parmesan cheese.

# Red Wine Risotto

❀ SERVES 4 AS A STARTER
❀ PREPARATION TIME: 20 MINUTES
❀ COOKING TIME: 25 MINUTES

500 ml (17 fl oz/2 cups) chicken stock
100 g (3½ oz) butter
1 onion, finely chopped
1 large garlic clove, crushed
2 tablespoons chopped thyme
220 g (7¾ oz/1 cup) risotto rice
500 ml (17 fl oz/2 cups) dry red wine
50 g (1¾ oz/½ cup) freshly grated
  parmesan cheese
Parmesan cheese, to sprinkle (if desired)

Pour the stock into a saucepan and bring to the boil. Reduce the heat, cover with a lid and keep at a low simmer.

Melt the butter in a large wide saucepan. Add the onion and garlic and cook until softened but not browned. Add the thyme and rice and stir until the rice is well coated. Season.

Add half the red wine and cook, stirring, until it has all been absorbed. Add 125 ml (4 fl oz/½ cup) of the hot stock and stir over medium heat until all the liquid is absorbed. Continue adding more stock, 125 ml (4 fl oz/½ cup) at a time until you have used half the stock. Add the remaining red wine to the risotto, stirring until it has been absorbed. Keep adding 125 ml (4 fl oz/½ cup) of the stock until all the liquid is absorbed and the rice is tender and creamy.

Remove the pan from the heat and stir in half the parmesan.

# Gorgonzola and Toasted Walnuts on Linguine

❀ SERVES 4
❀ PREPARATION TIME: 15 MINUTES
❀ COOKING TIME: 20 MINUTES

75 g (2½ oz/¾ cup) walnut halves
500 g (1 lb 2 oz) linguine
70 g (2½ oz) butter
150 g (5½ oz) gorgonzola cheese,
  crumbled
2 tablespoons pouring (whipping) cream
155 g (5½ oz/1 cup) fresh peas

Preheat the oven to 180°C (350°F/Gas 4). Lay the walnuts on a baking tray in a single layer and bake for about 5 minutes, until lightly toasted. Set the walnuts aside to cool.

Cook the linguine in a large saucepan of rapidly boiling salted water until *al dente*. Drain and return to the pan.

While the pasta is cooking, melt the butter in a small saucepan over low heat and add the gorgonzola, cream and peas. Stir gently for 5 minutes, or until the sauce has thickened. Season to taste. Add the sauce and the walnuts to the pasta and toss until well combined. Serve immediately, sprinkled with pepper.

*Red Wine Risotto*

# Orecchiette with Broccoli

🌸 SERVES 6

🌸 PREPARATION TIME: 5 MINUTES

🌸 COOKING TIME: 15 MINUTES

750 g (1 lb 10 oz) broccoli, cut into
   florets
450 g (1 lb) orecchiette
60 ml (2 fl oz/¼ cup) extra virgin olive
   oil
8 anchovy fillets
½ teaspoon dried chilli flakes
35 g (1¼ oz/⅓ cup) grated pecorino or
   parmesan cheese

Blanch the broccoli in a large saucepan of boiling salted water for 5 minutes, or until just tender. Remove with a slotted spoon, drain well and return the water to the boil. Cook the pasta in the boiling water until *al dente*, then drain well and return to the pan.

Meanwhile, heat the oil in a heavy-based frying pan and cook the anchovies over very low heat for about 1 minute. Add the chilli and broccoli. Increase the heat to medium and cook, stirring, for 5 minutes, or until the broccoli is well-coated and beginning to break apart. Season. Add to the pasta, add the cheese and toss.

# Spaghetti with Creamy Lemon Sauce

🌸 SERVES 4

🌸 PREPARATION TIME: 10 MINUTES

🌸 COOKING TIME: 20 MINUTES

500 g (1 lb 2 oz) spaghetti
250 ml (9 fl oz/1 cup) pouring
   (whipping) cream
185 ml (6 fl oz/¾ cup) chicken stock
1 tablespoon finely grated lemon zest, plus
   extra, to garnish
2 tablespoons finely chopped flat-leaf
   (Italian) parsley
2 tablespoons snipped chives

Cook the spaghetti in a large saucepan of rapidly boiling salted water until *al dente*. Drain and return to the pan.

While the spaghetti is cooking, combine the cream, chicken stock and lemon zest in a saucepan over medium heat. Bring to the boil, stirring occasionally. Reduce the heat and simmer gently for 10 minutes, or until the sauce is reduced and thickened slightly.

Add the sauce and herbs to the spaghetti and toss to combine. Serve immediately, garnished with extra lemon zest.

*Orecchiette with Broccoli*

# Herb~Filled Ravioli with Sage Butter

🌸 SERVES 4
🌸 PREPARATION TIME: 1 HOUR
🌸 COOKING TIME: 10 MINUTES

PASTA
300 g (10½ oz) plain (all-purpose) flour
3 eggs, beaten
60 ml (2 fl oz/¼ cup) olive oil
250 g (9 oz/1 cup) ricotta cheese
2 tablespoons freshly grated parmesan
    cheese
2 teaspoons snipped chives
1 tablespoon chopped flat-leaf (Italian)
    parsley
2 teaspoons chopped basil
1 teaspoon chopped thyme
shaved parmesan cheese, to garnish

SAGE BUTTER
200 g (7 oz) butter
12 sage leaves

To make the dough, sift the flour into a bowl and make a well in the centre. Gradually mix in the eggs and oil. Turn out onto a lightly floured surface and knead for 6 minutes, or until smooth. Cover with plastic wrap and leave for 30 minutes.

Mix together the ricotta, parmesan and herbs. Season.

Divide the dough into four even portions. Lightly flour a large work surface and using a floured long rolling pin, roll out one portion from the centre to the edge. Continue, always rolling from in front of you outwards. Rotate the dough often. Fold the dough in half and roll it out again. Continue this process seven times to make a smooth circle of pasta about 5 mm (¼ inch) thick. Roll this sheet out quickly and smoothly to a thickness of 2.5 mm (⅛ inch). Make four sheets of pasta, two slightly larger than the others. Cover with a tea towel. Spread one of the smaller sheets out on a work surface and place heaped teaspoons of ricotta filling at 5 cm (2 inch) intervals. Brush a little water between the filling along the cutting lines. Place a larger sheet on top and press the sheets together along the cutting lines. Cut the ravioli with a pastry wheel or knife and transfer to a floured baking tray. Repeat with the remaining dough and filling.

To make the sage butter, melt the butter over low heat in a small heavy-based saucepan. Pour the clear butter into another container and discard the remaining white sediment. Return the clarified butter to a pan and heat over medium heat. Add the sage leaves and cook until crisp. Drain on paper towels. Reserve the warm butter.

Cook the ravioli in batches in a large saucepan of salted simmering water for 5–6 minutes, or until tender. Remove with a slotted spoon. Top with warm sage butter and leaves and garnish with shaved parmesan.

NOTE: Don't cook the ravioli in rapidly boiling water or the squares will split and lose the filling.

# Scallops on Asian Risotto Cakes with Pesto

❀ SERVES 4
❀ PREPARATION TIME: 35 MINUTES
❀ COOKING TIME: 40 MINUTES

500 ml (17 fl oz/2 cups) vegetable stock
2 tablespoons mirin
1 lemon grass stem, white part only,
    bruised
2 makrut (kaffir lime) leaves
3 coriander (cilantro) roots
1 tablespoon fish sauce
20 g (¾ oz) butter
1 tablespoon peanut oil
3 red Asian shallots, thinly sliced
4 spring onions (scallions), chopped
3 garlic cloves, chopped
2 tablespoons finely chopped fresh ginger
1 teaspoon white pepper
140 g (5 oz/⅔ cup) risotto rice

PESTO
2 tablespoons toasted unsalted chopped
    peanuts
50 g (1¾ oz) chopped coriander (cilantro)
    leaves
2 garlic cloves, chopped
1 teaspoon finely chopped fresh ginger
½ teaspoon white papper
60 ml (2 fl oz/¼ cup) lime juice
1–2 teaspoons grated palm sugar (jaggery)
    or soft brown sugar
1 tablespoon fish sauce
1–2 tablespoons peanut oil
vegetable oil, for pan-frying
plain (all-purpose) flour, to dust
16 large white scallops without roe
lime slices, to serve
coriander (cilantro) leaves, to garnish

Combine the stock, mirin, lemon grass, makrut (kaffir lime) leaves, coriander roots, fish sauce and 250 ml (9 fl oz/1 cup) water in a saucepan, bring to the boil, then reduce the heat and keep at a simmer.

To make the risotto, heat the butter and peanut oil in a large saucepan over medium heat until bubbling. Add the shallot, spring onion, garlic, ginger and white pepper and cook for 2–3 minutes, or until fragrant and the onion is soft. Add the rice and stir until coated. Add 125 ml (4 fl oz/½ cup) of the stock (avoid the lemon grass and coriander roots). Stir constantly over medium heat until nearly all the liquid is absorbed. Continue adding the stock 125 ml (4 fl oz/½ cup) at a time, stirring constantly, for 20–25 minutes, or until all the stock is absorbed and the rice is tender and creamy. Remove from the heat, cool, then cover and refrigerate for 3 hours, or until cold.

To make the pesto, combine the peanuts, coriander leaves, garlic, ginger and the white pepper in a blender or food processor and process until finely chopped. With the motor running, slowly add the lime juice, palm sugar, fish sauce and peanut oil and process until smooth — you might not need all the oil.

Divide the risotto into four balls, then mould into patties. Cover and refrigerate for 10 minutes. Heat the vegetable oil in a large frying pan over medium heat. Dust the patties with the flour and cook in batches for 2 minutes on each side, or until crisp. Drain on paper towels. Cover and keep warm.

Heat a little vegetable oil in a clean frying pan over high heat. Cook the scallops in batches for 1 minute on each side. Serve a cake with four scallops, some pesto and lime slices. Garnish with the coriander leaves.

# Fettucine with Zucchini and Crisp-Fried Basil

🌺 SERVES 6

🌺 PREPARATION TIME: 15 MINUTES

🌺 COOKING TIME: 15 MINUTES

250 ml (9 fl oz/1 cup) olive oil
handful basil leaves
500 g (1 lb 2 oz) fettucine or tagliatelle
500 g (1 lb 2 oz) zucchini (courgettes)
60 g (2¼ oz) butter
2 garlic cloves, crushed
75 g (2¾ oz/¾ cup) freshly grated
    parmesan cheese

To crisp-fry the basil leaves, heat the oil in a small frying pan, add two leaves at a time and cook for 1 minute, or until crisp. Remove with a slotted spoon and drain on paper towel. Repeat with the remaining basil leaves.

Cook the fettucine in a large saucepan of rapidly boiling salted water until *al dente*. Drain and return to the pan.

While the pasta is cooking, grate the zucchini. Melt the butter in a deep heavy-based saucepan over low heat until foaming. Add the garlic and cook for 1 minute. Add the zucchini and cook, stirring occasionally, for 1–2 minutes, or until softened. Add to the hot pasta. Add the parmesan and toss well. Serve the pasta garnished with the crisp basil leaves.

# Blue Cheese Tagliatelle

🌺 SERVES 6

🌺 PREPARATION TIME: 15 MINUTES

🌺 COOKING TIME: 20 MINUTES

30 g (1 oz) butter
2 zucchini (courgettes), sliced
1 garlic clove, crushed
100 ml (3½ fl oz) dry white wine
100 g (3½ oz) blue cheese, crumbled
300 ml (10½ fl oz) pouring (whipping)
    cream
500 g (1 lb 2 oz) white or green tagliatelle
2–3 tablespoons freshly grated parmesan
    cheese
chopped flat-leaf (Italian) parsley,
    to garnish

Melt the butter in a frying pan. Add the zucchini and garlic and cook until the zucchini is tender. Stir in the wine, blue cheese, cream and a pinch of black pepper. Simmer for 10 minutes.

Meanwhile, cook the tagliatelle in a large saucepan of rapidly boiling salted water until *al dente*. Drain, rinse under warm water and drain again. Return the pasta to the pan. Add the sauce and toss through the pasta for a few minutes over low heat. Serve sprinkled with the parmesan and parsley.

*Fettucine with Zucchini and Crisp-Fried Basil*

# Tomato and Cheese Risotto Cakes

🌼 SERVES 6
🌼 PREPARATION TIME: 30 MINUTES
🌼 COOKING TIME: 40 MINUTES

1 small onion
30 g (1 oz) sun-dried (sun-blushed)
  tomatoes
30 g (1 oz) mozzarella cheese
810 ml (28$^1$/$_4$ fl oz/3$^1$/$_4$ cups) vegetable
  stock
1 tablespoon olive oil
20 g ($^3$/$_4$ oz) butter
275 g (9$^3$/$_4$ oz/1$^1$/$_4$ cups) short-grain rice
35 g (1$^1$/$_4$ oz/$^1$/$_3$ cup) freshly grated
  parmesan cheese
vegetable oil, for deep-frying
70 g (2$^1$/$_2$ oz) mixed salad leaves, to serve

Finely chop the onion. Chop the sun-dried tomatoes and cut the mozzarella cheese into 1 cm ($^1$/$_2$ inch) cubes.

Bring the stock to the boil in a small saucepan. Reduce the heat, cover and keep gently simmering.

Heat the olive oil and butter in a heavy-based saucepan. Add the onion and stir over medium heat for 3 minutes, or until golden. Add the rice. Reduce the heat to low and stir for 3 minutes, or until the rice is lightly golden. Add a quarter of the stock to the pan. Stir for 5 minutes, or until all the liquid has been absorbed. Repeat the process until all the stock has been added and the rice is almost tender, stirring constantly. Stir in the parmesan. Remove from the heat, transfer to a bowl to cool and refrigerate for 1 hour.

With wet hands, roll 2 tablespoons of the rice mixture into a ball. Make an indentation in the ball and press in a cube of mozzarella and a couple of pieces of sun-dried tomato. Reshape the ball to cover the indentation, then flatten slightly to a disc shape. Repeat the process with the remaining mixture. Refrigerate for 15 minutes.

Fill a deep-fryer or large heavy-based saucepan one-third full of vegetable oil and heat to 180°C (350°F), or until a cube of bread dropped into the oil browns in 15 seconds. Gently lower risotto cakes, a few at a time, into the oil. Cook for 1–2 minutes, or until golden brown. Remove with a slotted spoon and drain on paper towel. Serve the risotto cakes with salad leaves.

# Orecchiette with Tuna, Lemon and Caper Sauce

❁ SERVES 4
❁ PREPARATION TIME: 10 MINUTES
❁ COOKING TIME: 20 MINUTES

500 g (1 lb 2 oz) orecchiette
30 g (1 oz) butter
1 garlic clove, crushed
1 onion, finely chopped
425 g (15 oz) tinned tuna in brine,
    drained
2 tablespoons lemon juice
250 ml (9 fl oz/1 cup) pouring
    (whipping) cream
2 tablespoons chopped flat-leaf (Italian)
    parsley
1 tablespoon capers, drained
1/4 teaspoon cayenne pepper (optional)
caperberries, to garnish (optional)

Cook the orecchiette in a large saucepan of rapidly boiling salted water until *al dente*. Drain and return to the pan.

Melt the butter in a saucepan and cook the garlic and onion for 1–2 minutes. Add the tuna, lemon juice, cream, half the parsley and the capers. Season with black pepper and cayenne pepper, if using. Simmer over low heat for 5 minutes.

Add the tuna sauce to the pasta and toss until thoroughly combined. Serve the pasta sprinkled with the remaining parsley. Garnish with caperberries, if desired.

# Creamy Prawns with Fettucine

❁ SERVES 4
❁ PREPARATION TIME: 30 MINUTES
❁ COOKING TIME: 20 MINUTES

500 g (1 lb 2 oz) fettucine
500 g (1 lb 2 oz) raw prawns (shrimp)
30 g (1 oz) butter
1 tablespoon olive oil
6 spring onions (scallions), chopped
1 garlic clove, crushed
250 ml (9 fl oz/1 cup) pouring
    (whipping) cream
2 tablespoons chopped flat-leaf (Italian)
    parsley, to serve

Cook the fettucine in a large saucepan of rapidly boiling water until *al dente*. Drain and return to the pan.

Peel the prawns and gently pull out the dark vein from each prawn back, starting from the head end. Heat the butter and oil in a frying pan, add the spring onion and garlic and stir over low heat for 1 minute. Add the prawns and cook for 2–3 minutes, or until the flesh changes colour. Remove the prawns from the pan and set aside. Add the cream to the pan and bring to the boil. Reduce the heat and simmer until the sauce begins to thicken. Return the prawns to the pan, season to taste, and simmer for 1 minute.

Add the prawns and sauce to the warm fettucine and toss gently. Serve sprinkled with chopped parsley.

*Orecchiette with Tuna, Lemon and Caper Sauce*

# Penne alla Napolitana

🌸 SERVES 4–6
🌸 PREPARATION TIME: 20 MINUTES
🌸 COOKING TIME: 25 MINUTES

2 tablespoons olive oil
1 onion, finely chopped
2–3 garlic cloves, finely chopped
1 small carrot, finely diced
1 celery stalk, finely diced
800 g (1 lb 12 oz) tinned peeled, chopped
    tomatoes or 1 kg (2 lb 4 oz) ripe
    tomatoes, peeled and chopped
1 tablespoon tomato paste (concentrated
    purée)
3 tablespoons shredded basil
500 g (1 lb 2 oz) penne
freshly grated parmesan cheese, to serve
    (optional)

Heat the oil in a large frying pan. Add the onion and garlic and cook for 2 minutes, or until golden. Add the carrot and celery and cook for a further 2 minutes.

Add the tomato and tomato paste. Simmer for 20 minutes, or until the sauce thickens, stirring occasionally. Stir in the basil and season to taste.

While the sauce is cooking, cook the pasta in a large saucepan of rapidly boiling salted water until *al dente*. Drain well and return to the pan. Add the sauce to the pasta and mix well. Serve with freshly grated parmesan cheese, if desired.

# Spaghetti Puttanesca

🌸 SERVES 6
🌸 PREPARATION TIME: 15 MINUTES
🌸 COOKING TIME: 20 MINUTES

80 ml (2½ fl oz/⅓ cup) olive oil
2 onions, finely chopped
3 garlic cloves, finely chopped
½ teaspoon dried chilli flakes
6 large ripe tomatoes, diced
4 tablespoons capers, rinsed and squeezed
    dry
8 anchovy fillets in oil, drained and
    chopped
150 g (5½ oz) kalamata olives
3 tablespoons chopped flat-leaf (Italian)
    parsley
375 g (13 oz) spaghetti

Heat the olive oil in a saucepan, add the onion and cook over medium heat for 5 minutes. Add the garlic and chilli flakes to the pan and cook for 30 seconds. Add the tomato, capers and anchovies. Simmer over low heat for 10–15 minutes, or until the sauce is thick and pulpy. Stir the olives and parsley through the sauce.

While the sauce is cooking, cook the spaghetti in a large saucepan of rapidly boiling salted water until *al dente*. Drain and return to the pan.

Add the sauce to the pasta and stir it through. Season to taste and serve immediately.

*Penne alla Napolitana*

# Mushroom Risotto

❀ SERVES 6–8
❀ PREPARATION TIME: 10 MINUTES
❀ COOKING TIME: 1 HOUR

20 g (³/₄ oz) dried porcini mushrooms
1 litre (35 fl oz/4 cups) chicken or
   vegetable stock
2 tablespoons olive oil
100 g (3½ oz) butter, chopped
650 g (1 lb 7 oz) small cap or Swiss
   brown mushrooms, stems trimmed,
   sliced
3 garlic cloves, crushed
80 ml (2½ fl oz/⅓ cup) dry white
   vermouth
1 onion, finely chopped
440 g (15½ oz/2 cups) risotto rice
150 g (5½ oz/1½ cups) freshly grated
   parmesan cheese

Soak the porcini mushrooms in 500 ml (17 fl oz/ 2 cups) warm water for 30 minutes. Drain, retaining the liquid. Chop mushrooms, then pour the liquid through a fine sieve lined with a paper towel.

Put the stock and the mushroom liquid together in a saucepan. Bring to the boil, then reduce the heat, cover and keep at a low simmer.

Heat half the oil and 40 g (1½ oz) of the butter in a frying pan over high heat. Add all the mushrooms and the garlic to the pan. Cook, stirring, for 10 minutes, or until soft. Reduce the heat to low and cook for a further 5 minutes. Increase the heat, add the vermouth and cook for 2–3 minutes, until evaporated. Set aside.

Heat the remaining olive oil and 20 g (³/₄ oz) butter in a saucepan. Add the onion and cook for 10 minutes, or until soft. Add the rice and stir for 1–2 minutes, or until coated. Add 125 ml (4 fl oz/½ cup) stock to the pan and stir constantly over medium heat until all the liquid is absorbed. Continue adding more stock, 125 ml (4 fl oz/½ cup) at a time, stirring, for 20–25 minutes, or until tender. Remove from the heat and stir in the mushrooms, parmesan and the remaining butter. Season to taste.

# Gnocchi Romana

❀ SERVES 4
❀ PREPARATION TIME: 20 MINUTES
❀ COOKING TIME: 40 MINUTES

750 ml (26 fl oz/3 cups) milk
1/2 teaspoon freshly grated nutmeg
85 g (3 oz/2/3 cup) semolina
1 egg, beaten
150 g (51/2 oz/11/2 cups) freshly grated
   parmesan cheese
60 g (21/4 oz) butter, melted
125 ml (4 fl oz/1/2 cup) pouring
   (whipping) cream
75 g (23/4 oz/1/2 cup) freshly grated
   mozzarella cheese

Line a deep Swiss roll tin (jelly roll tin) with baking paper. Combine the milk and half the nutmeg in a saucepan and season to taste. Bring to the boil, reduce the heat and gradually stir in the semolina. Cook, stirring occasionally, for 5–10 minutes, or until the semolina is very stiff.

Remove the pan from the heat, add the egg and 100 g (31/2 oz/1 cup) of the parmesan. Stir to combine and then spread the mixture in the prepared tin. Refrigerate for 1 hour, or until the mixture is firm.

Preheat the oven to 180°C (350°F/Gas 4). Lightly grease a shallow casserole dish. Cut the semolina into rounds using a floured 4 cm (11/2 inch) cutter and arrange in the dish.

Pour the melted butter over the top, followed by the cream. Combine the remaining grated parmesan with the mozzarella cheese and sprinkle on the rounds. Sprinkle with the remaining nutmeg. Bake for 20–25 minutes, or until the mixture is golden.

# Risi e Bisi

❁ SERVES 4
❁ PREPARATION TIME: 15 MINUTES
❁ COOKING TIME: 25 MINUTES

1.5 litres (52 fl oz/6 cups) chicken or
    vegetable stock
2 teaspoons olive oil
40 g (1½ oz) butter
1 small onion, finely chopped
80 g (2¾ oz) pancetta, cubed
2 tablespoons chopped flat-leaf (Italian)
    parsley
375 g (13 oz) young peas
220 g (7¾ oz/1 cup) risotto rice
50 g (1¾ oz/½ cup) freshly grated
    parmesan cheese

Pour the stock into a saucepan and bring to the boil.
Reduce the heat, cover with a lid and keep at a low
simmer.

Heat the oil and half the butter in a large wide heavy-
based saucepan and cook the onion and pancetta over
low heat for 5 minutes until softened. Stir in the parsley
and peas and add two ladlefuls of the stock. Simmer for
6–8 minutes.

Add the rice and the remaining stock. Simmer until the
rice is *al dente* and most of the stock has been absorbed.
Stir in the remaining butter and the parmesan, season
and serve.

# Garlic Bucatini

❁ SERVES 4
❁ PREPARATION TIME: 10 MINUTES
❁ COOKING TIME: 20 MINUTES

500 g (1 lb 2 oz) bucatini or penne
80 ml (2½ fl oz/⅓ cup) olive oil
8 garlic cloves, crushed
2 tablespoons chopped flat-leaf (Italian)
    parsley
freshly grated parmesan cheese, to serve

Cook the bucatini in a large saucepan of rapidly boiling
salted water until *al dente*. Drain and return to the pan.

Heat the olive oil over low heat in a frying pan and
add the garlic. Cook for 1 minute before removing from
the heat. Add the garlic, oil and the parsley to the pasta
and toss to distribute thoroughly. Serve with parmesan
cheese.

*Risi e Bisi*

# Spaghetti Marinara

❀ SERVES 6

❀ PREPARATION TIME: 40 MINUTES

❀ COOKING TIME: 50 MINUTES

12 mussels

TOMATO SAUCE
2 tablespoons olive oil
1 onion, finely diced
1 carrot, sliced
1 red chilli, seeded and chopped
2 garlic cloves, crushed
425 g (15 oz) tinned crushed tomatoes
125 ml (4 fl oz/½ cup) dry white wine
1 teaspoon sugar
pinch cayenne pepper

60 ml (2 fl oz/¼ cup) white wine
60 ml (2 fl oz/¼ cup) fish stock
1 garlic clove, crushed
375 g (13 oz) spaghetti
30 g (1 oz) butter
125 g (4½ oz) small squid tubes, sliced
125 g (4½ oz) boneless white fish fillets, cubed
200 g (7 oz) raw prawns (shrimp), peeled and deveined
1 large handful flat-leaf (Italian) parsley, chopped
200 g (7 oz) tinned clams (vongole), drained

Scrub the mussels with a stiff brush and pull out the hairy beards. Discard any broken mussels, or open ones that don't close when tapped on the bench. Rinse well.

To make the tomato sauce, heat the oil in a saucepan, add the onion and carrot and stir over medium heat for about 10 minutes, or until the vegetables are lightly browned. Add the chilli, garlic, tomato, white wine, sugar and cayenne pepper. Simmer for 30 minutes, stirring occasionally.

Meanwhile, heat the wine with the stock and garlic in a large saucepan and add the unopened mussels. Cover the pan and shake it over high heat for 3–5 minutes. After 3 minutes, start removing any opened mussels and set them aside. After 5 minutes discard any unopened mussels and reserve the wine mixture.

Cook the pasta in a large saucepan of rapidly boiling salted water until *al dente*. Drain and keep warm.

Melt the butter in a frying pan, add the squid rings, fish and prawns and stir-fry for 2 minutes. Set aside. Add the reserved wine mixture, mussels, squid, fish, prawns, parsley and clams to the tomato sauce and reheat gently. Gently combine the sauce with the pasta and serve at once.

# Spiced Carrot and Feta Gnocchi

- SERVES 6–8
- PREPARATION TIME: 20 MINUTES
- COOKING TIME: 10 MINUTES

1 kg (2 lb 4 oz) carrots
200 g (7 oz) feta cheese, crumbled
280 g (10 oz/2 1/4 cups) plain (all-purpose) flour
1/4 teaspoon ground nutmeg
1/4 teaspoon garam masala
1 egg, lightly beaten

MINTED CREAM SAUCE
30 g (1 oz) butter
2 garlic cloves, crushed
2 spring onions (scallions), sliced
250 ml (9 fl oz/1 cup) pouring (whipping) cream
2 tablespoons shredded mint

Cut the carrots into large pieces and steam, boil or microwave until tender. Drain and allow to cool slightly before transferring to a food processor.

Process the carrot and the feta together until smooth. Transfer the mixture to a large bowl. Stir in the sifted flour, spices and egg, and mix to form a soft dough.

Lightly coat your fingertips with flour and shape teaspoons of the mixture into flat circles.

To make the minted cream sauce, melt the butter in a frying pan, add the garlic and spring onion and cook over medium heat for 3 minutes, or until the garlic is soft and golden. Add the cream, bring to the boil then reduce the heat and simmer for 3 minutes, or until the cream has thickened slightly. Remove from the heat and stir through the mint.

Meanwhile, cook the gnocchi, in batches, in a large saucepan of boiling salted water for about 2 minutes, or until they float to the surface. Use a slotted spoon to transfer to warmed serving plates. Drizzle the minted cream sauce over the gnocchi and serve.

*NOTE: This mixture is not as firm as some other gnocchi recipes. Make sure the dough is put on a lightly floured surface and keep your fingertips coated in flour when you are shaping the gnocchi.*

# Tagliatelle with Chicken Livers and Cream

❋ SERVES 4
❋ PREPARATION TIME: 20 MINUTES
❋ COOKING TIME: 15 MINUTES

375 g (13 oz) tagliatelle
300 g (10½ oz) chicken livers
2 tablespoons olive oil
1 onion, finely chopped
1 garlic clove, crushed
250 ml (9 fl oz/1 cup) pouring
    (whipping) cream
1 tablespoon snipped chives
1 teaspoon wholegrain mustard
2 eggs, beaten
freshly grated parmesan cheese, to serve
snipped chives, to serve

Cook the tagliatelle in a large saucepan of rapidly boiling salted water until *al dente*. Drain and return to the pan.

While the pasta is cooking, trim any green or discoloured parts from the chicken livers, then slice them. Heat the olive oil in a large frying pan. Add the onion and garlic and stir over low heat until the onion is tender.

Add the chicken liver to the pan and cook gently for 2–3 minutes. Remove from the heat and stir in the cream, chives and mustard and season to taste. Return to the heat and bring to the boil. Add the beaten eggs and stir quickly to combine. Remove from the heat.

Add the sauce to the hot pasta and toss well to combine. Serve sprinkled with parmesan and snipped chives.

# Linguine Pesto

🌸 SERVES 4–6
🌸 PREPARATION TIME: 15 MINUTES
🌸 COOKING TIME: 15 MINUTES

100 g (3½ oz) basil
2 garlic cloves, crushed
40 g (1½ oz/¼ cup) pine nuts, toasted
185 ml (6 fl oz/¾ cup) olive oil
50 g (1¾ oz/½ cup) freshly grated
    parmesan cheese, plus extra, to serve
500 g (1 lb 2 oz) linguine

Process the basil, garlic and pine nuts together in a food processor. With the motor running, add the oil in a steady stream until mixed to a smooth paste. Transfer to a bowl, stir in the parmesan and season to taste.

Cook the pasta in a large saucepan of rapidly boiling salted water until *al dente*. Drain and return to the pan. Toss enough of the pesto through the pasta to coat it well. Serve sprinkled with parmesan.

NOTE: Refrigerate any leftover pesto in an airtight jar for up to a week. Cover the surface with a layer of oil. Freeze for up to 1 month.

# Spaghetti Vongole

🌸 SERVES 4
🌸 PREPARATION TIME: 25 MINUTES
🌸 COOKING TIME: 35 MINUTES

1 kg (2 lb 4 oz) small clams (vongole) in
    shell or 750 g (1 lb 10 oz) tinned clams
    (vongole) in brine
1 tablespoon lemon juice
80 ml (2½ fl oz/⅓ cup) olive oil
3 garlic cloves, crushed
850 g (1 lb 14 oz) tinned crushed
    tomatoes
250 g (9 oz) spaghetti
4 tablespoons chopped flat-leaf (Italian)
    parsley

If using fresh clams, clean thoroughly. Place in a large saucepan with the lemon juice. Cover the pan and shake over medium heat for 7–8 minutes until the shells open, discarding any that don't open. Remove the clam flesh from the shell of the opened clams and set aside; discard the empty shells. If using canned clams, drain, rinse well and set aside.

Heat the oil in a large saucepan. Add the garlic and cook over low heat for 5 minutes. Add the tomato and stir to combine. Bring to the boil and simmer, covered, for 20 minutes. Add freshly ground black pepper, to taste, and the clams, and stir until heated through.

While the sauce is cooking, cook the spaghetti in a large saucepan of rapidly boiling salted water until *al dente*. Drain and return to the pan. Gently stir in the sauce and the chopped parsley until combined.

*Linguine Pesto*

# Fennel Risotto Balls with Cheesy Filling

🌸 SERVES 6–8
🌸 PREPARATION TIME: 30 MINUTES
🌸 COOKING TIME: 50 MINUTES

1.5 litres (52 fl oz/6 cups) vegetable stock
1 tablespoon oil
30 g (1 oz) butter
2 garlic cloves, crushed
1 onion, finely chopped
2 fennel bulbs, thinly sliced
1 tablespoon balsamic vinegar
125 ml (4 fl oz/½ cup) dry white wine
440 g (15½ oz/2 cups) risotto rice
50 g (1¾ oz/½ cup) freshly grated
    parmesan cheese
25 g (1 oz/½ cup) snipped chives
1 egg, lightly beaten
150 g (5½ oz) sun-dried (sun-blushed)
    tomatoes, chopped
100 g (3½ oz) mozzarella cheese, cubed
80 g (2¾ oz/½ cup) frozen peas, thawed
60 g (2¼ oz/½ cup) plain (all-purpose)
    flour, seasoned
3 eggs, extra
200 g (7 oz/2 cups) dry breadcrumbs
vegetable oil, for deep-frying

Pour the stock into a saucepan and bring to the boil. Reduce the heat, cover with a lid and keep at a low simmer.

Heat the oil and butter in a large saucepan and cook the garlic and onion over medium heat for 3 minutes, or until softened but not browned. Add the fennel and cook for 10 minutes, or until it starts to caramelize. Add the vinegar and wine, increase the heat and boil until the liquid evaporates. Stir in the rice until well coated.

Add 125 ml (4 fl oz/½ cup) hot stock, stirring constantly over medium heat until the liquid is absorbed. Continue adding more stock, 125 ml (4 fl oz/½ cup) at a time, stirring, for 20–25 minutes, or until all the stock is absorbed and the rice is tender and creamy.

Remove from the heat and stir in the parmesan, chives, egg and sun-dried tomato. Transfer to a bowl, cover and cool. Put the mozzarella and peas in a bowl and mash together. Season well.

Put the flour in one bowl, the extra eggs in another and the breadcrumbs in a third. Lightly beat the eggs. With wet hands, shape the risotto into 14 even balls. Flatten each ball out, slightly indenting the centre. Put a heaped teaspoon of the pea mash into the indentation, then shape the rice around the filling to form a ball. Roll each ball in seasoned flour, then dip in the extra egg and roll in breadcrumbs. Place on a foil-covered tray and refrigerate for 30 minutes.

Fill a deep-fat fryer or large saucepan one-third full of oil and heat to 180°C (350°F), or until a cube of bread dropped into the oil browns in 15 seconds. Cook the risotto balls in batches for 5 minutes, or until golden and crisp and the cheese has melted inside. Drain on crumpled paper towels and season with salt. If the cheese has not melted by the end of the cooking time, cook the balls on a tray in a 180°C (350°F/Gas 4) oven for 5 minutes. Serve with a salad.

# Creamy Seafood Ravioli

❀ SERVES 4
❀ PREPARATION TIME: 1 HOUR
❀ COOKING TIME: 30 MINUTES

## PASTA DOUGH

250 g (9 oz/2 cups) plain (all-purpose)
    flour
3 eggs
1 tablespoon olive oil

## FILLING

50 g (1¾ oz) butter, softened
3 garlic cloves, finely chopped
2 tablespoons finely chopped flat-leaf
    (Italian) parsley
100 g (3½ oz) scallops, cleaned and finely
    chopped
100 g (3½ oz) raw prawn (shrimp) meat,
    finely chopped
1 egg yolk

## SAUCE

70 g (2½ oz) butter
3 tablespoons plain (all-purpose) flour
375 ml (13 fl oz/1½ cups) milk
300 ml (10½ fl oz) pouring (whipping)
    cream
125 ml (4 fl oz/½ cup) dry white wine
50 g (1¾ oz/½ cup) freshly grated
    parmesan cheese
2 tablespoons chopped flat-leaf (Italian)
    parsley

To make the pasta dough, sift the flour and a pinch of salt into a bowl and make a well in the centre. Whisk the eggs, oil and 1 tablespoon water in a bowl, then add gradually to the flour and mix to a firm dough. Gather into a ball.

Knead on a lightly floured surface for 5 minutes, or until smooth and elastic. Transfer to a lightly oiled bowl, cover with plastic wrap and set aside for 30 minutes.

To make the filling, mix together the butter, garlic, parsley, scallops and prawn meat. Set aside.

Roll out a quarter of the pasta dough at a time until very thin (each portion of dough should be roughly 10 cm/4 inches wide when rolled). Place 1 teaspoonful of filling at 5 cm (2 inch) intervals down one side of each strip. Whisk the egg yolk with 60 ml (2 fl oz/¼ cup) water. Brush along one side of the dough and between the filling. Fold the dough over the filling to meet the other side. Repeat with the remaining filling and dough. Press the edges of the dough together firmly to seal.

Cut between the mounds with a knife or a fluted pastry cutter. Cook, in batches, in a large saucepan of rapidly boiling salted water for 6 minutes each batch. Drain well and return to the pan to keep warm.

To make the sauce, melt the butter in a saucepan, add the flour and cook over low heat for 2 minutes. Remove from the heat and stir in the combined milk, cream and wine. Cook over low heat until the sauce begins to thicken, stirring constantly. Bring to the boil and simmer gently for 5 minutes. Add the parmesan and parsley and stir until combined. Remove from the heat, add to the ravioli and toss well.

NOTE: The pasta dough is set aside for 30 minutes to let the gluten in the flour relax. If you don't do this, you run the risk of making tough pasta.

# Spaghettini with Garlic and Chilli

🌿 SERVES 4–6
🌿 PREPARATION TIME: 10 MINUTES
🌿 COOKING TIME: 20 MINUTES

500 g (1 lb 2 oz) spaghettini
125 ml (4 fl oz/ 1/2 cup) extra virgin olive
    oil
2–3 garlic cloves, finely chopped
1–2 red chillies, seeded and finely chopped
3 tablespoons chopped flat-leaf (Italian)
    parsley
freshly grated parmesan cheese, to serve

Cook the spaghettini in a large saucepan of rapidly boiling salted water until *al dente*. Drain and return to the pan.

Meanwhile, heat the extra virgin olive oil in a large frying pan. Add the garlic and chilli, and cook over very low heat for 2–3 minutes, or until the garlic is golden. Take care not to burn the garlic or chilli as this will make the sauce bitter.

Toss the parsley and the warmed oil, garlic and chilli mixture through the pasta. Season well. Serve with the parmesan.

# Cheese Tortellini with Nutty Herb Sauce

🌿 SERVES 4–6
🌿 PREPARATION TIME: 15 MINUTES
🌿 COOKING TIME: 15 MINUTES

500 g (1 lb 2 oz) ricotta-filled fresh or
    dried tortellini or ravioli
60 g (2 1/4 oz) butter
100 g (3 1/2 oz) walnuts, finely chopped
100 g (3 1/2 oz/ 2/3 cup) pine nuts
2 tablespoons chopped flat-leaf (Italian)
    parsley
2 teaspoons thyme
60 g (2 1/4 oz/ 1/4 cup) ricotta cheese
60 ml (2 fl oz/ 1/4 cup) pouring (whipping)
    cream

Add the pasta to a large saucepan of rapidly boiling salted water and cook until *al dente*. Drain and return to the pan.

To make the sauce, heat the butter in a heavy-based frying pan over medium heat until foaming. Add the walnuts and pine nuts and stir for 5 minutes, or until golden brown. Add the parsley, thyme and season.

Beat the ricotta with the cream. Add the sauce to the pasta and toss well to combine. Top with a dollop of ricotta cream. Serve immediately.

*Spaghettini with Garlic and Chilli*

# Spinach and Ricotta Gnocchi

🌸 SERVES 4–6
🌸 PREPARATION TIME: 45 MINUTES
🌸 COOKING TIME: 30 MINUTES

4 slices white bread
125 ml (4 fl oz/½ cup) milk
500 g (1 lb 2 oz) frozen spinach, thawed
250 g (9 oz/1 cup) ricotta cheese
2 eggs
50 g (1¾ oz/½ cup) freshly grated
   parmesan cheese
30 g (1 oz/¼ cup) plain (all-purpose)
   flour
parmesan cheese shavings, to serve

Remove the crusts from the bread and soak the bread in the milk for 10 minutes. Squeeze out all the excess liquid. Squeeze the excess liquid from the spinach.

Combine the bread in a bowl with the spinach, ricotta cheese, eggs and parmesan, then season. Use a fork to mix thoroughly. Cover and refrigerate for 1 hour.

Lightly dust your hands in flour. Roll heaped teaspoons of the mixture into dumplings. Lower batches of the gnocchi into a large saucepan of boiling salted water. Cook for about 2 minutes, or until the gnocchi rise to the surface. Transfer to serving plates. Drizzle with foaming butter, if you wish, and serve with the parmesan shavings.

# Pasta and Spinach Timbales

🌸 SERVES 6
🌸 PREPARATION TIME: 25 MINUTES
🌸 COOKING TIME: 45 MINUTES

30 g (1 oz) butter
1 tablespoon olive oil
1 onion, chopped
500 g (1 lb 2 oz) English spinach, steamed
   and well-drained
8 eggs, lightly beaten
250 ml (9 oz/1 cup) pouring (whipping)
   cream
100 g (3½ oz) spaghetti or taglioni,
   cooked
60 g (2¼ oz/½ cup) grated cheddar
   cheese
50 g (1¾ oz/½ cup) freshly grated
   parmesan cheese

Preheat the oven to 180°C (350°F/Gas 4). Brush six 250 ml (9 oz/1 cup) ramekins or dariole moulds with some melted butter or oil. Line the bases with baking paper. Heat the butter and oil together in a frying pan. Add the onion and stir over low heat until the onion is tender. Add the spinach and cook for 1 minute. Remove from the heat and leave to cool. Whisk in the eggs and cream. Stir in the spaghetti or taglioni and grated cheeses then season to taste. Stir well and spoon into the prepared ramekins.

Place the ramekins in an ovenproof dish. Pour boiling water into the dish to come halfway up the sides of the ramekins. Bake for 30–35 minutes, or until set. Near the end of cooking time, test the timbales with the point of a knife. When cooked, the knife should come out clean.

Allow the timbales to rest for 15 minutes before turning them out. Run the point of a knife around the edge of each ramekin. Invert onto serving plates.

*Spinach and Ricotta Gnocchi*

# pastry

# Pumpkin Tarts

❀ SERVES 6
❀ PREPARATION TIME: 30 MINUTES
❀ COOKING TIME: 20 MINUTES

250 g (9 oz/2 cups) plain (all-purpose)
    flour
125 g (4½ oz) chilled butter, cubed
80 ml (2½ fl oz/⅓ cup) iced water
1.25 kg (2 lb 12 oz) pumpkin (winter
    squash), cut into 6 cm (2½ inch) pieces
125 g (4½ oz/½ cup) sour cream or
    cream cheese
sweet chilli sauce, to serve

Sift the flour and a pinch of salt into a large bowl. Using your fingertips, rub in the butter until the mixture resembles fine breadcrumbs. Make a well in the centre, add the iced water and mix with a flat-bladed knife, using a cutting action, until the mixture comes together in beads. Gently gather the dough together and lift out onto a lightly floured work surface. Press into a ball, then flatten slightly into a disc, wrap in plastic wrap and refrigerate for 30 minutes.

Preheat the oven to 200°C (400°F/Gas 6). Divide the pastry into six portions, roll each one out and fit into a 10 cm (4 inch) pie dish. Trim the edge and prick the bases all over with a fork. Bake on a baking tray for 15 minutes, or until lightly golden, pressing down any pastry that puffs up. Cool, then remove from the tins.

Meanwhile, steam the pumpkin for about 15 minutes, or until tender.

Place a tablespoon of sour cream or cream cheese in the middle of each pastry case and pile the pumpkin pieces on top. Season and drizzle with sweet chilli sauce to taste. Return to the oven for a couple of minutes to heat through. Serve immediately.

# Sweet Potato, Feta and Pine Nut Strudel

※ SERVES 6
※ PREPARATION TIME: 25 MINUTES
※ COOKING TIME: 55 MINUTES

450 g (1 lb) sweet potato, cut into 2 cm
   (³⁄₄ inch) cubes
1 tablespoon olive oil
80 g (2³⁄₄ oz/¹⁄₂ cup) pine nuts, toasted
   (see Notes)
250 g (9 oz) feta cheese, crumbled
2 tablespoons chopped basil
4 spring onions (scallions), chopped
40 g (1¹⁄₂ oz) butter, melted
2 tablespoons olive oil, extra, for brushing
7 sheets filo pastry
2–3 teaspoons sesame seeds

Preheat the oven to 180°C (350°F/Gas 4). Brush the sweet potato with oil and bake for 20 minutes, or until softened and slightly coloured. Transfer to a bowl and cool. Add the pine nuts, feta, basil and spring onion to the bowl, mix gently and season to taste.

Mix together the butter and extra oil. Remove one sheet of filo and cover the rest with a damp tea towel (dish towel) to prevent them from drying out. Brush each sheet of filo with the butter mixture and layer them into a pile.

Spread the prepared filling in the centre of the filo, covering an area about 10 x 30 cm (4 x 12 inches). Fold the sides of the pastry into the centre, then tuck in the ends. Carefully turn the strudel over and place on a baking tray, seam side down. Lightly brush the top with the butter mixture and sprinkle with sesame seeds. Bake for 35 minutes, or until the pastry is crisp and golden. Serve warm.

NOTES: You can use 450 g (1 lb) of pumpkin (winter squash) instead of the sweet potato.
   To toast pine nuts, dry-fry them in a frying pan, stirring and watching them constantly so they don't burn.

# Fish Wellington

🌸 SERVES 6

🌸 PREPARATION TIME: 30 MINUTES

🌸 COOKING TIME: 1 HOUR 15 MINUTES

40 g (1½ oz) butter

3 onions, thinly sliced

2 x 300 g (10½ oz) skinless firm white
    fish fillets (each 30 cm/12 inches long)

½ teaspoon sweet paprika

2 red capsicums (peppers), quartered,
    seeded and membrane removed

1 large eggplant (aubergine) (320 g/
    11¼ oz), cut into 1 cm (½ inch)
    thick slices

olive oil, for brushing

375 g (13 oz) block puff pastry, thawed

35 g (1¼ oz/⅓ cup) dry breadcrumbs

1 egg, lightly beaten

250 g (9 oz/1 cup) plain yoghurt

1–2 tablespoons chopped dill

Melt the butter in a saucepan, add the onion and stir to coat. Cover and cook over low heat, stirring occasionally, for 15 minutes. Uncover and cook, stirring, for 15 minutes, or until the onion is very soft and lightly browned. Cool, then season to taste.

Rub one side of each fish fillet with the paprika. Place one on top of the other, with the paprika on the outside. If the fillets have a thin and a thick end, sandwich together so the thickness is even along the length (thin ends on top of thick ends).

Cook the capsicum quarters, skin side up, under a hot grill (broiler) until the skin blackens and blisters. Cool in a plastic bag, then peel. Place the eggplant on a greased baking tray and brush with oil. Sprinkle with salt and pepper. Grill until golden, then turn to brown the other side.

Preheat the oven to 220°C (425°F/Gas 7). Roll the pastry out on a lightly floured surface until large enough to enclose the fish, about 25 x 35 cm (10 x 14 inches). The pastry size and shape will be determined by the fish. Sprinkle the breadcrumbs lengthways along the centre of the pastry and place the fish over the breadcrumbs. Top with the onion, then a layer of capsicum, followed by a layer of eggplant.

Brush the pastry edges with the egg. Fold the pastry over, pinching firmly together to seal. Use any trimmings to decorate. Brush with more egg, then bake for 30 minutes. Cover loosely with foil if the pastry is overbrowning. Slice to serve.

Mix the yoghurt and dill with a little salt and pepper in a bowl. Serve with the Wellington.

# Cheese and Mushroom Pies

40 g (1½ oz) butter

2 garlic cloves, crushed

500 g (1 lb 2 oz) button mushrooms, sliced

1 small red capsicum (pepper), seeded, membrane removed and finely chopped

160 g (5¾ oz/⅔ cup) sour cream

3 teaspoons wholegrain mustard

130 g (4¾ oz/1 cup) finely grated gruyère or cheddar cheese

6 sheets ready-rolled puff pastry

1 egg, lightly beaten, to glaze

Preheat the oven to 190°C (375°F/Gas 5). Lightly grease two baking trays. Heat the butter in a large frying pan. Add the garlic and mushroom and cook over medium heat, stirring occasionally, until the mushroom is tender and the liquid has evaporated. Remove from the heat and cool. Stir in the capsicum.

Combine the sour cream, mustard and half the cheese. Cut twelve circles of pastry with a 14 cm (5½ inch) cutter. Spread the cream mixture over six circles, leaving a 1 cm (½ inch) border. Top each with mushroom mixture and 2 teaspoons of the remaining cheese. Brush the outer edges with the beaten egg then place the reserved pastry rounds on top of the filling, sealing the edges with a fork. Brush the tops of the pastry with the egg and sprinkle with the remaining cheese. Place the pies on the oven trays and bake for 20 minutes, or until lightly browned and puffed.

# Tapenade and Anchovy Tartlets

500 g (1 lb 2 oz) block ready-made puff pastry, thawed

125 g (4½ oz/½ cup) ready-made tapenade

50 g (1¾ oz) tinned anchovies, drained

35 g (1¼ oz/⅓ cup) freshly grated parmesan cheese

75 g (2¾ oz/½ cup) freshly grated mozzarella cheese

Divide the pastry into two portions. Roll each portion between two sheets of baking paper. If making four tartlets, cut out two 12 cm (4½ inch) circles of pastry from each portion, or for two long tartlets roll each portion of pastry into a rectangle 12 x 25 cm (4½ x 10 inches).

Preheat the oven to 200°C (400°F/Gas 6). Spread the tapenade evenly over the pastry shapes, leaving a 1.5 cm (⅝ inch) border. Cut the anchovies into thin strips and arrange them over the top of the tapenade. Sprinkle the parmesan and mozzarella over the top. Bake for 10 minutes, or until risen and golden.

*Cheese and Mushroom Pies*

# Roast Capsicum Rice Tarts

🌸 SERVES 6

🌸 PREPARATION TIME: 45 MINUTES

🌸 COOKING TIME: 1 HOUR 5 MINUTES

1 litre (35 fl oz/4 cups) vegetable stock
20 g ($^3$/$_4$ oz) butter
95 g (3$^1$/$_2$ oz/$^1$/$_2$ cup) wild rice
140 g (5 oz/$^2$/$_3$ cup) short-grain brown
    rice
1 egg, lightly beaten with 1 egg yolk
50 g (1$^3$/$_4$ oz/$^1$/$_2$ cup) freshly grated
    parmesan cheese
2 green capsicums (peppers)
2 red capsicums (peppers)
2 yellow capsicums (peppers)
150 g (5$^1$/$_2$ oz) camembert cheese, thinly
    sliced
2 tablespoons oregano

Grease six 10 cm (4 inch) loose-based fluted flan (tart) tins. Pour the stock into a saucepan and bring to the boil. Reduce the heat, cover and keep at a low simmer.

Melt the butter in a large saucepan over low heat, then stir in the rice until well coated. Add 125 ml (4 fl oz/ $^1$/$_2$ cup) of the hot stock to the rice, stirring well. Increase the heat to medium and add the remaining stock, 250 ml (9 fl oz/1 cup) at a time, stirring, until it has been absorbed. This will take about 30 minutes. Remove from the heat and cool. Add the egg and parmesan and season to taste.

Divide the rice mixture among the prepared flan tins and press it around the base and sides. Allow to cool completely. Preheat the oven to 200°C (400°F/Gas 6).

Cut the capsicums in half and remove the seeds and membrane, then cut into large, flattish pieces. Grill (broil) or hold over a gas flame until the skin blackens and blisters. Put on a cutting board, cover with a tea towel (dish towel) and allow to cool. Peel off the skin and cut the flesh into smaller pieces.

Put the camembert slices in the bottom of the rice-lined tins and divide the capsicum evenly among the tarts. Bake for 30 minutes. Sprinkle the oregano over the top and serve hot.

# Vol~au~Vents

🌼 MAKES 4
🌼 PREPARATION TIME: 20 MINUTES
🌼 COOKING TIME: 30 MINUTES

250 g (9 oz) block ready-made puff
  pastry, thawed
1 egg, lightly beaten

SAUCE AND FILLING
40 g (1¹/₂ oz) butter
2 spring onions (scallions), finely chopped
2 tablespoons plain (all-purpose) flour
375 ml (13 fl oz/1¹/₂ cups) milk
your choice of filling (see Note)

Preheat the oven to 220°C (425°F/Gas 7). Line a baking tray with baking paper. Roll out the pastry to a 20 cm (8 inch) square. Cut four circles of pastry with a 10 cm (4 inch) cutter. Place the rounds onto the tray and cut 6 cm (2¹/₂ inch) circles into the centre of the rounds with a cutter, taking care not to cut right through the pastry. Place the baking tray in the refrigerator for 15 minutes.

Using a floured knife blade, 'knock up' the sides of each pastry round by making even indentations about 1 cm (¹/₂ inch) apart around the circumference. This should allow even rising of the pastry as it cooks. The dough can be made ahead of time up to this stage and frozen until needed. Carefully brush the pastry with the egg, avoiding the 'knocked up' edge as any glaze spilt on the sides will stop the pastry from rising. Bake for 15–20 minutes, or until the pastry has risen and is golden brown and crisp. Cool on a wire rack. Remove the centre from each pastry circle and pull out and discard any partially cooked pastry from the centre. The pastry can be returned to the oven for 2 minutes to dry out if the centre is undercooked. The pastry cases are now ready to be filled with a hot filling before serving.

To make the sauce, melt the butter in a saucepan, add the spring onion and stir over low heat for 2 minutes, or until soft. Add the flour and stir for 2 minutes, or until lightly golden. Gradually add the milk, stirring until smooth. Stir constantly over medium heat for 4 minutes, or until the mixture boils and thickens. Season well. Remove and stir in your choice of filling (see Note).

NOTE: Add 350 g (12 oz) of any of the following to your white sauce: sliced, cooked mushrooms; peeled, deveined and cooked prawns; chopped, cooked chicken breast; poached, flaked salmon; cooked and dressed crabmeat; oysters; steamed asparagus spears.

# Tunisian Brik

🌺 SERVES 2
🌺 PREPARATION TIME: 30 MINUTES
🌺 COOKING TIME: 20 MINUTES

30 g (1 oz) butter
1 small onion, finely chopped
200 g (7 oz) tinned tuna in oil, drained
1 tablespoon tiny capers, rinsed and
    chopped
2 tablespoons finely chopped flat-leaf
    (Italian) parsley
2 tablespoons grated parmesan cheese
6 sheets filo pastry
30 g (1 oz) butter, extra, melted
2 small eggs

Preheat the oven to 200°C (400°F/Gas 6). Melt the butter in a small frying pan and cook the onion over low heat for 5 minutes, or until soft but not brown. Combine the onion, tuna, capers, parsley and parmesan in a bowl and season.

Cut the filo pastry sheets in half widthways. Layer four of the half sheets together, brushing each with melted butter. Keep the remaining pastry covered with a damp tea towel (dish towel). Spoon half the tuna mixture onto one end of the buttered pastry, leaving a border. Make a well in the centre of the mixture and break an egg into the well, being careful to leave it whole.

Layer two more sheets of filo together, brushing with melted butter, and place on top of the tuna and egg. Fold in the pastry sides, then roll into a firm parcel, keeping the egg whole. Place on a lightly greased baking tray and brush with melted butter. Repeat with the remaining pastry, filling and egg. Bake for 15 minutes, or until the pastry is golden brown. Serve warm or at room temperature.

# Smoked Cod Flan

🌼 SERVES 6

🌼 PREPARATION TIME: 30 MINUTES

🌼 COOKING TIME: 55 MINUTES

PASTRY

125 g (4½ oz/1 cup) plain (all-purpose)
　　flour
60 g (2¼ oz) butter, chopped
1 egg, lightly beaten
1 tablespoon lemon juice
1–2 tablespoons iced water

FILLING

300 g (10½ oz) smoked cod or haddock
　　fillets
3 eggs, lightly beaten
125 ml (4 fl oz/½ cup) pouring
　　(whipping) cream
60 g (2¼ oz/½ cup) grated cheddar
　　cheese
1 tablespoon chopped dill

Preheat the oven to 210°C (415°F/Gas 6–7). Lightly grease a 22 cm (8½ inch) diameter loose-based fluted flan (tart) tin.

To make the pastry, sift the flour into a large bowl. Using your fingertips, rub in the butter until the mixture resembles fine breadcrumbs. Make a well in the centre and add the egg, lemon juice and most of the iced water. Mix with a flat-bladed knife, using a cutting action, until the mixture comes together in beads. Add more water if the dough is too dry. Gently gather the dough together into a ball, flatten into a disc and wrap in plastic wrap. Refrigerate for 20 minutes.

Roll out the dough between two sheets of baking paper until large enough to cover the base and side of the tin. Remove the top sheet of paper and put the pastry in the tin, pressing into the sides. Line with baking paper large enough to cover the base and sides and spread a layer of baking beads or uncooked rice over the top. Bake for 10 minutes, remove the paper and beads and bake for another 5 minutes, or until golden. Remove and cool slightly. Reduce the oven to 180°C (350°F/Gas 4).

To make the filling, put the cod in a frying pan and cover with water. Bring to the boil, reduce the heat and simmer for 10–15 minutes, or until the cod flakes easily when tested with a fork. Drain on crumpled paper towel, then allow to cool.

Flake the cod into small pieces, using a fork. Combine the eggs, cream, cheddar and dill in a bowl, add the cod and mix well. Spoon into the pastry shell and bake for 40 minutes, or until set. Serve the flan hot or cold with lemon or lime wedges and a green salad.

# Cherry Tomato and Pesto Tart

❀ SERVES 4
❀ PREPARATION TIME: 15 MINUTES
❀ COOKING TIME: 10 MINUTES

500 g (1 lb 2 oz) block ready-made
    puff pastry, thawed
125 g (4½ oz/½ cup) ready-made pesto
375 g (13 oz) cherry tomatoes
2 spring onions (scallions), finely sliced
extra virgin olive oil, to drizzle
spring onion (scallion) slices, to garnish

Divide the pastry into two portions. Roll each portion between two sheets of baking paper. If making four tartlets, cut out two 12 cm (4½ inch) circles of pastry from each portion, or for two long tartlets roll each portion of pastry into a rectangle 12 x 25 cm (4½ x 10 inches).

Preheat the oven to 200°C (400°F/Gas 6). Spread the pesto over the pastry shapes, leaving a 1.5 cm (⅝ inch) border. Top with the cherry tomatoes and finely sliced spring onion. Season and bake for 10 minutes, or until golden. Drizzle with extra virgin olive oil and garnish with the spring onion slices. Serve warm or hot.

# Free-Form Prawn Pies

❀ SERVES 4
❀ PREPARATION TIME: 20 MINUTES
❀ COOKING TIME: 30 MINUTES

250 g (9 oz/2 cups) plain (all-purpose) flour
125 g (4½ oz) chilled butter, cubed
60 ml (2 fl oz/¼ cup) iced water
1 tablespoon oil
5 cm (2 inch) piece fresh ginger, grated
3 garlic cloves, crushed
1 kg (2 lb 4 oz) raw prawns (shrimp), peeled
80 ml (2½ fl oz/⅓ cup) sweet chilli sauce
80 ml (2½ fl oz/⅓ cup) lime juice
80 ml (2½ fl oz/⅓ cup) thick (double/
    heavy) cream
25 g (1 oz) chopped coriander (cilantro)
1 egg yolk, lightly beaten, to glaze
lime zest strips, to garnish

Sift the flour into a bowl. Rub in the butter. Add the water and mix. Gather the dough together and lift out onto a lightly floured surface. Press into a ball and flatten into a disc. Wrap in plastic wrap and chill for 15 minutes. Preheat the oven to 200°C (400°F/Gas 6). Grease two baking trays.

Heat the oil in a large frying pan and fry the ginger, garlic and prawns for 2–3 minutes. Remove the prawns and set aside. Add the chilli sauce, lime juice and cream to the pan and simmer until the sauce has reduced by about one-third. Return the prawns to the pan and add the coriander. Cool. Divide the pastry into four and roll out each portion, between sheets of baking paper, into a 20 cm (8 inch) circle. Divide the filling into four and place a portion in the centre of each pastry circle, leaving a wide border. Fold the edges over the filling. Brush the pastry with the egg yolk. Bake for 25 minutes, or until golden. Serve with lime zest.

*Cherry Tomato and Pesto Tart*

# Pissaladière

❀ SERVES 8
❀ PREPARATION TIME: 50 MINUTES
❀ COOKING TIME: 2 HOUR

2 teaspoons dried yeast
1 teaspoon caster (superfine) sugar
310 g (11 oz/2½ cups) white strong flour
2 tablespoons milk powder
1 tablespoon vegetable oil

TOMATO AND ONION TOPPING
80 ml (2½ fl oz/⅓ cup) olive oil
3–4 garlic cloves, finely chopped
6 onions, cut into thin rings
425 g (15 oz) tinned chopped tomatoes
1 tablespoon tomato paste (concentrated
    purée)
15 g (½ oz) chopped flat-leaf (Italian)
    parsley
1 tablespoon chopped thyme
3 x 50 g (1¾ oz) tins anchovy fillets,
    drained and halved lengthways
36 niçoise olives

Grease two 30 cm (12 inch) pizza trays. Put the yeast, sugar and 250 ml (9 fl oz/1 cup) warm water in a bowl and stir well. Leave in a warm place for 10 minutes.

Sift 250 g (9 oz/2 cups) of the flour, the milk powder and ½ teaspoon salt into a bowl and make a well in the centre. Add the oil and yeast mixture and mix. Turn out onto a floured surface and knead for 10 minutes, gradually adding small amounts of the remaining flour, until the dough is smooth and elastic.

Place in an oiled bowl and brush the surface with oil. Cover with plastic wrap and leave in a warm place for 30 minutes, or until doubled in size.

To make the topping, heat the oil in a saucepan. Add the garlic and onion and cook, covered, over low heat for about 40 minutes, stirring frequently. Uncover and cook, stirring frequently, for another 30 minutes. Cool.

Put the tomatoes in a saucepan and cook over medium heat, stirring frequently, for 20 minutes, or until thick and reduced to about 250 ml (9 fl oz/1 cup). Remove from the heat and stir in the tomato paste and herbs. Season to taste. Cool, then stir into the onion mixture.

Preheat the oven to 220°C (425°F/Gas 7). Punch down the dough, then turn out onto a floured surface and knead for 2 minutes. Divide in half. Return one half to the bowl and cover. Roll the other out to a 30 cm (12 inch) circle and press into the tray. Brush with olive oil. Spread half the onion and tomato mixture evenly over the dough, leaving a small border. Arrange half the anchovy fillets over the top in a lattice pattern and place an olive in each square. Repeat with the rest of the dough and topping. Bake for 15–20 minutes, or until the dough is cooked through and lightly browned.

NOTE: If your oven can accommodate both pissaladière at once and you want to cook them together, the cooking time will be longer. Rotate the trays towards the end of cooking time.

# Tomato and Bocconcini Flan

✿ SERVES 6
✿ PREPARATION TIME: 30 MINUTES
✿ COOKING TIME: 50 MINUTES

185 g (6½ oz/1½ cups) plain
    (all-purpose) flour
100 g (3½ oz) butter, chopped
1 egg
2 tablespoons cold water
5–6 roma (plum) tomatoes
1 tablespoon olive oil
8 bocconcini (fresh baby mozzarella
    cheese) (about 220 g/7¾ oz), sliced
6 spring onions (scallions), chopped
2 tablespoons chopped rosemary

Combine the flour and butter in a food processor. Process for 10 seconds, or until fine and crumbly. Combine the egg and water in a small bowl. With the motor constantly running, gradually add to the flour mixture and process until the mixture just comes together. Turn out onto a lightly floured surface and knead to form a smooth dough. Refrigerate, covered with plastic wrap, for 20 minutes.

Preheat the oven to 210°C (415°F/Gas 6–7). On a floured board, roll the pastry to fit a 23 cm (9 inch) round, loose-based flan (tart) tin. Ease the pastry into the tin and trim the edges. Cut a sheet of baking paper to cover the pastry-lined tin. Place over the pastry then spread a layer of baking beads or uncooked rice evenly over the paper. Bake for 15 minutes, then remove the paper and beads and bake for another 10 minutes, or until the pastry case is lightly golden, then cool. Reduce the oven to 180°C (350°F/Gas 4).

Cut the tomatoes in half, sprinkle with salt and drizzle with the oil. Place in an ovenproof dish, cut side up and bake for 15 minutes. Arrange the tomatoes, cut side up, over the pastry. Place the bocconcini slices and spring onion between the tomatoes. Scatter with rosemary and season. Bake for 10 minutes. Remove from the oven and cool for 10 minutes before serving.

# Goat's Cheese Galette

* SERVES 6
* PREPARATION TIME: 20 MINUTES
* COOKING TIME: 1 HOUR 15 MINUTES

PASTRY
125 g (4½ oz/1 cup) plain (all-purpose)
    flour
60 ml (2 fl oz/¼ cup) olive oil

FILLING
1 tablespoon olive oil
2 onions, thinly sliced
1 teaspoon thyme
125 g (4½ oz/½ cup) ricotta cheese
100 g (3½ oz) goat's cheese
2 tablespoons pitted niçoise olives
1 egg, beaten
60 ml (2 fl oz/¼ cup) pouring (whipping)
    cream

To make the pastry, sift the flour and a pinch of salt into a bowl and make a well in the centre. Add the olive oil and mix with a flat-bladed knife until crumbly. Gradually add 60–80 ml (2–2½ fl oz/¼–⅓ cup) water until the mixture comes together. Remove and pat together to form a disc. Refrigerate for 30 minutes.

Meanwhile, to make the filling, heat the oil in a frying pan. Add the onion, cover and cook for 30 minutes. Season and stir in half the thyme. Cool.

Preheat the oven to 180°C (350°F/Gas 4). Lightly flour the workbench and roll out the pastry to a 30 cm (12 inch) circle. Then put on a heated baking tray. Evenly spread the onion over the pastry, leaving a 2 cm (¾ inch) border. Sprinkle the ricotta and goat's cheese evenly over the onion. Put the olives over the cheeses, then sprinkle with the remaining thyme. Fold the pastry border in to the edge of the filling, pleating as you go.

Combine the egg and cream, then pour over the filling. Bake in the lower half of the oven for 45 minutes, or until the pastry is golden.

# Mushroom, Asparagus and Feta Tart

SERVES 4

PREPARATION TIME: 30 MINUTES

COOKING TIME: 25 MINUTES

500 g (1 lb 2 oz) block ready-made puff
    pastry, thawed
2 tablespoons oil
400 g (14 oz) sliced, small button
    mushrooms
100 g (3½ oz) thin asparagus spears,
    woody ends trimmed
2 tablespoons chopped flat-leaf (Italian)
    parsley
200 g (7 oz) chopped feta cheese

Divide the pastry into two and roll each portion between two sheets of baking paper. If making four tartlets, cut out two 12 cm (4½ inch) circles of pastry from each portion, or for two long tartlets roll each portion of pastry into a rectangle 12 x 25 cm (4½ x 10 inches). Preheat the oven to 200°C (400°F/Gas 6).

Heat the oil in a frying pan, add the mushroom and asparagus and stir until softened. Remove from the heat and add the parsley and feta. Stir and season. Spoon onto the pastry bases, leaving a 1.5 cm (⅝ inch) border. Bake in the top half of the oven for about 10–15 minutes, or until risen and brown. Serve warm or hot.

# Sour Cream Tomato Pizza

SERVES 4

PREPARATION TIME: 30 MINUTES

COOKING TIME: 40 MINUTES

1 teaspoon dried yeast
1 teaspoon caster (superfine) sugar
250 g (9 oz/2 cups) plain (all-purpose)
    flour
125 ml (4 fl oz/½ cup) olive oil

TOPPING
125 g (4½ oz/½ cup) sour cream
90 g (3¼ oz/⅓ cup) ricotta cheese
2 tablespoons chopped herbs (such as
    basil, lemon thyme, sage)
2 tablespoons oil
2 onions, thinly sliced
5 ripe tomatoes, sliced
2 garlic cloves, thinly sliced
50 g (1¾ oz) marinated niçoise olives
10 lemon thyme sprigs, chopped

Preheat the oven to 200°C (400°F/Gas 6). To make the base, put the yeast, sugar and 170 ml (5½ fl oz/⅔ cup) warm water into a bowl and mix to dissolve the sugar. Leave in a warm, draught-free place for 10 minutes, or until bubbles appear on the surface. The mixture should be frothy and slightly increased in volume. If your yeast doesn't foam, it is dead, so you will have to discard it and start again.

Put the flour and a pinch of salt into a food processor, add the oil and the yeast mixture with the motor running and process until it forms a rough dough. Turn out onto a lightly floured surface and knead until smooth. Place in a lightly oiled bowl, cover and allow to rest in a warm area for 1½ hours, or until doubled in size. Punch down the dough and remove from the bowl. Knead and roll out to a 30 cm (12 inch) circle, or four 14 cm (5½ inch) circles and place on a non-stick baking tray.

To make the topping, combine the sour cream, ricotta and herbs. Spread over the pizza base, leaving a 1 cm (½ inch) border.

Heat the oil in a frying pan, add the onions and cook for 10 minutes, or until caramelized. Cool slightly, spoon over the ricotta mixture and top with the tomato, garlic, olives, lemon thyme and some freshly cracked black pepper. Bake in the top half of the oven for 15–30 minutes, depending on size, until the base is crisp and golden.

# Turkish Pizza

❀ MAKES 8
❀ PREPARATION TIME: 25 MINUTES
❀ COOKING TIME: 45 MINUTES

1 teaspoon dried yeast
½ teaspoon sugar
225 g (8 oz) plain (all-purpose) flour
80 ml (2½ fl oz/⅓ cup) olive oil
250 g (9 oz) onions, finely chopped
500 g (1 lb 2 oz) minced (ground) lamb
2 garlic cloves
1 teaspoon ground cinnamon
1½ teaspoons ground cumin
½ teaspoon cayenne pepper
60 g (2¼ oz/¼ cup) tomato paste
    (concentrated purée)
400 g (14 oz) tinned good-quality crushed
    tomatoes
50 g (1¾ oz/⅓ cup) pine nuts
3 tablespoons chopped coriander (cilantro)
Greek-style yoghurt, to serve

Mix the yeast, sugar and 60 ml (2 fl oz/¼ cup) warm water in a bowl. Leave in a warm, draught-free place for 10 minutes, or until bubbles appear on the surface. The mixture should be frothy and slightly increased in volume. If your yeast doesn't foam, it is dead, so you will have to discard it and start again.

Sift the flour and 1 teaspoon salt into a bowl, stir in the yeast mixture, 1 tablespoon of the oil and 100 ml (3½ fl oz) warm water. Mix to form a soft dough, then turn onto a floured board and knead for 10 minutes, or until smooth. Place in an oiled bowl, cover and leave in a warm place for 1 hour, or until doubled in size.

Heat 2 tablespoons of the oil in a frying pan over low heat and cook the onion for 5 minutes, or until soft but not golden. Add the lamb and cook for 10 minutes, or until brown. Add the garlic and spices, tomato paste and tomato. Cook for 15 minutes, until quite dry. Add half the pine nuts and 2 tablespoons of the coriander. Season, then leave to cool.

Preheat the oven to 210°C (415°F/Gas 6–7). Grease two baking trays.

Knock down the dough, then turn out onto a floured surface. Form into eight portions and roll each into a 12 x 18 cm (4½ x 7 inch) oval. Place on the trays. Divide the lamb mixture evenly among them and spread, leaving a small border. Sprinkle with the remaining pine nuts. Brush the edges with oil. Roll the uncovered dough over to cover the outer edges of the filling. Pinch the sides together at each end. Brush with oil. Bake for 15 minutes, or until golden. Sprinkle with the remaining coriander and serve with yoghurt.

# Crab Quiche

❀ SERVES 4–6
❀ PREPARATION TIME: 40 MINUTES
❀ COOKING TIME: 1 HOUR 5 MINUTES

PASTRY
220 g (7¾ oz/1¾ cups) plain (all-
    purpose) flour
100 g (3½ oz) chilled butter, chopped
2 tablespoons iced water

FILLING
20 g (¾ oz) butter
1 onion, thinly sliced
200 g (7 oz) tinned crabmeat, drained
3 eggs
185 ml (6 fl oz/¾ cup) pouring
    (whipping) cream
90 g (3¼ oz/¾ cup) grated cheddar
    cheese
dill sprigs (optional)

To make the pastry, sift the flour into a bowl. Using your fingertips, rub in the butter until the mixture resembles fine breadcrumbs. Make a well in the centre and add the iced water. Mix with a flat-bladed knife, using a cutting action, until the mixture comes together in beads. Add a little more water if the dough is too dry. Turn out onto a lightly floured work surface and gather into a ball. Divide the pastry into two portions. Cover with plastic wrap and refrigerate for 20 minutes. Preheat the oven to 190°C (375°F/Gas 5). Grease two 12 cm (4½ inches) round, 4 cm (1½ inches) deep flan (tart) tins.

Roll out both portions of pastry between two sheets of baking paper to fit the tins. Lift the pastry into the tins and press it well into the sides. Trim off any excess by rolling a rolling pin across the top of the tin. Refrigerate the pastry for 20 minutes. Cover the shells with baking paper, fill evenly with baking beads or uncooked rice and bake for 15 minutes, or until the pastry is dried out and golden. Remove the paper and beads and cool slightly. Reduce the oven to 180°C (350°F/Gas 4).

To make the filling, melt the butter in a small frying pan and cook the onion until just soft. Remove from the pan and drain on paper towel. Squeeze out any excess moisture from the crabmeat. Spread the onion and crabmeat over the cooled pastry cases, arranging the crab in the centre of each quiche. Mix the eggs, cream and cheddar in a bowl. Pour into the pastry cases and, if you like, top with some dill sprigs. Bake for 40 minutes, or until lightly golden and set.

# Feta and Olive Herb Pie

❀ SERVES 4–6
❀ PREPARATION TIME: 40 MINUTES
❀ COOKING TIME: 45 MINUTES

PASTRY

1 teaspoon sugar
2 teaspoons dried yeast
1 tablespoon olive oil
60 g (2¼ oz/½ cup) plain (all-purpose)
    flour
125 g (4½ oz/1 cup) self-raising flour

FILLING

1 tablespoon olive oil
1 onion, sliced
1 teaspoon sugar
15 g (½ oz) flat-leaf (Italian) parsley,
    chopped
1 rosemary sprig, chopped
3 thyme sprigs, chopped
5 basil leaves, torn
40 g (1½ oz/¼ cup) pine nuts, toasted
    (see Note)
1 garlic clove, crushed
175 g (6 oz) feta cheese, crumbled
30 g (1 oz) pitted olives, chopped

Dissolve half the sugar in 125 ml (4 fl oz/½ cup) warm water and sprinkle the yeast over the top. Leave in a warm, draught-free place for 10 minutes, or until bubbles appear on the surface. If your yeast doesn't foam, it is dead and you will have to start again. Mix the yeast mixture with the oil.

Sift the flours and ½ teaspoon salt into a large bowl. Make a well in the centre and pour in the yeast mixture. Mix well and knead on a lightly floured board until smooth. Cut the dough in half, then roll each half into a 20 cm (8 inch) circle. Place one circle on a lightly greased baking tray, the other on a baking tray covered with baking paper. Cover the circles with a tea towel and put in a warm place for 10–15 minutes, or until doubled in size. Preheat the oven to 200°C (400°F/Gas 6).

To make the filling, heat the oil in a frying pan, add the onion and for 10 minutes, or until golden brown. Sprinkle with the remaining sugar and cook for a further 5 minutes, or until caramelized. Transfer to a bowl and mix with the herbs, pine nuts, garlic, feta and olives. Spread the mixture over the pastry on the greased tray. Brush the edge with water and put the second pastry circle on top, using the paper to help lift it over. Press the edges together to seal and pinch together to form a pattern. Cut a few slits in the top of the pastry to allow steam to escape. Bake for 30–35 minutes, or until crisp and golden brown. Serve warm, cut into wedges.

NOTE: To toast pine nuts, you can dry-fry them in a frying pan, stirring and watching them constantly so they don't burn.

# Herbed Fish Tartlets

❋ MAKES 8
❋ PREPARATION TIME: 40 MINUTES
❋ COOKING TIME: 45 MINUTES

PASTRY
155 g (5½ oz/1¼ cups) plain
    (all-purpose) flour
90 g (3¼ oz) butter, chopped
1 tablespoon chopped thyme
1 tablespoon chopped dill
2 tablespoons chopped flat-leaf (Italian)
    parsley
90 g (3¼ oz) cheddar cheese, finely grated
60–80 ml (2–2½ fl oz/¼–⅓ cup) iced
    water

FILLING
400 g (14 oz) skinless firm white fish
    fillets
2 spring onions (scallions), finely chopped
2 tablespoons chopped flat-leaf (Italian)
    parsley
60 g (2¼ oz/½ cup) finely grated
    cheddar cheese
2 eggs
125 ml (4 fl oz/½ cup) pouring
    (whipping) cream

Lightly grease eight 10 cm (4 inch) round fluted flan (tart) tins. Sift the flour into a large bowl. Using your fingertips, rub in the butter until the mixture resembles fine breadcrumbs. Stir in the herbs and cheddar. Make a well in the centre. Add almost all the water and mix with a flat-bladed knife, using a cutting action, until the mixture comes together in beads. Add more water if the dough is too dry. Gather together and form into a ball. Wrap in plastic wrap and refrigerate for 15 minutes.

Preheat the oven to 210°C (415°F/Gas 6–7). Divide the pastry into eight portions. Roll each on a lightly floured work surface, large enough to fit the tins. Ease into the tins, pressing into the sides. Trim the edges with a sharp knife or by rolling a rolling pin across the tops of the tins. Place the tins on a baking tray. Cover each pastry case with a sheet of baking paper. Spread a single layer of baking beads or uncooked rice evenly over the base. Bake for 10 minutes, then remove the paper and beads and bake for another 10 minutes, or until lightly browned. Cool.

To make the filling, put the fish in a frying pan and add enough water to cover. Bring to the boil, reduce the heat and simmer gently for 3 minutes. Remove from the pan with a slotted spoon and drain on crumpled paper towel. Allow to cool, then flake with a fork. Divide among the cases and sprinkle with the combined spring onion, parsley and cheddar. Whisk together the eggs and cream, then pour over the fish. Bake for 25 minutes, or until set and golden brown. Serve immediately.

NOTE: Smoked fish can be used. You can make the recipe in a 23 cm (9 inch) flan (tart) tin. Cooking time may be longer but check after 25 minutes.

# Potato and Onion Pizza

❀ SERVES 4

❀ PREPARATION TIME: 40 MINUTES

❀ COOKING TIME: 45 MINUTES

2 teaspoons dried yeast
1/2 teaspoon sugar
185 g (6 1/2 oz/1 1/2 cups) white strong
    flour
150 g (5 1/2 oz/1 cup) wholemeal (whole-
    wheat) plain (all-purpose) flour
1 tablespoon olive oil

TOPPING
1 large red capsicum (pepper)
1 potato
1 large onion, sliced
125 g (4 1/2 oz) soft goat's cheese,
    crumbled into small pieces
35 g (1 1/4 oz/1/4 cup) capers
1 tablespoon dried oregano
1 teaspoon olive oil

Mix the yeast, sugar, a pinch of salt and 250 ml
(9 fl oz/1 cup) warm water in a bowl. Leave in a warm,
draught-free place for 10 minutes, or until bubbles
appear on the surface. The mixture should be frothy
and slightly increased in volume. If your yeast doesn't
foam, it is dead, so you will have to discard it and
start again.

Sift both flours into a bowl. Make a well in the centre,
add the yeast mixture and mix to a firm dough. Knead
on a lightly floured surface for 5 minutes, or until
smooth. Place in a lightly oiled bowl, cover with plastic
wrap or a damp tea towel (dish towel) and leave in a
warm, draught-free place for 1–1 1/2 hours, or until
doubled in size.

Preheat the oven to 200°C (400°F/Gas 6). Brush a
30 cm (12 inch) pizza tray with oil. Punch down the
dough and knead for 2 minutes. Roll out to a 35 cm
(14 inch) round. Put the dough on the tray and tuck
the edge over to form a rim.

To make the topping, cut the red capsicum into large
flattish pieces and remove the membrane and seeds.
Place, skin side up, under a hot grill (broiler) until
blackened. Cool in a plastic bag, then peel away the
skin and cut the flesh into narrow strips.

Cut the potato into paper-thin slices and arrange over
the base with the capsicum, onion and half the cheese.
Sprinkle with the capers, oregano and 1 teaspoon
cracked pepper and drizzle with oil. Brush the crust
edge with oil and bake for 20 minutes. Add the
remaining cheese and bake for 15–20 minutes, or
until the crust has browned. Serve in wedges.

# Moroccan Chicken Pie

❀ SERVES 6–8

❀ PREPARATION TIME: 30 MINUTES

❀ COOKING TIME: 1 HOUR 20 MINUTES

200 g (7 oz) butter
1.5 kg (3 lb 5 oz) chicken, cut into
    4 portions
1 large onion, finely chopped
3 teaspoons ground cinnamon
1 teaspoon ground ginger
2 teaspoons ground cumin
1/4 teaspoon cayenne pepper
1/2 teaspoon ground turmeric
1/2 teaspoon saffron threads soaked in
    2 tablespoons warm water
125 ml (4 fl oz/1/2 cup) chicken stock
4 eggs, lightly beaten
25 g (1 oz) chopped coriander (cilantro)
3 tablespoons chopped flat-leaf (Italian)
    parsley
50 g (1¾ oz/1/3 cup) chopped almonds
30 g (1 oz/1/4 cup) icing (confectioners')
    sugar
375 g (13 oz) filo pastry
icing (confectioners') sugar, extra, to dust

Preheat the oven to 180°C (350°F/Gas 4). Grease a 30 cm (12 inch) pizza tray.

Melt 40 g (1 1/2 oz) of the butter in a large frying pan. Add the chicken, onion, 2 teaspoons of the cinnamon, all the other spices and the stock. Season, cover and simmer for 30 minutes, or until the chicken is cooked through.

Remove the chicken from the sauce. When cool enough to handle, remove the meat from the bones, discard the skin and bones and shred the meat into thin strips.

Bring the liquid in the pan to a simmer and add the eggs. Cook the mixture, stirring constantly, until the eggs are cooked and the mixture is quite dry. Add the chicken, coriander and parsley, season well and mix. Remove from the heat.

Bake the almonds on a baking tray until golden brown. Cool slightly, then blend in a food processor or spice grinder with the icing sugar and remaining cinnamon until they resemble coarse crumbs.

Melt the remaining butter. Place a sheet of filo on the pizza tray and brush with melted butter. Place another sheet on top in a pinwheel effect and brush with butter. Continue brushing and layering until you have used eight sheets. Put the chicken mixture on top and sprinkle with the almond mixture.

Fold the overlapping filo over the top of the filling. Place a sheet of filo over the top and brush with butter. Continue to layer buttered filo over the top in the same pinwheel effect until you have used eight sheets. Tuck the overhanging edges under the pie to form a neat round parcel. Brush well with the remaining butter. Bake the pie for 40–45 minutes, or until cooked through and golden. Dust with icing sugar before serving.

# index

Published in 2009 by Murdoch Books Pty Limited

Murdoch Books Australia
Pier 8/9
23 Hickson Road
Millers Point NSW 2000
Phone: +61 (0) 2 8220 2000
Fax: +61 (0) 2 8220 2558
www.murdochbooks.com.au

Murdoch Books UK Limited
Erico House, 6th Floor
93–99 Upper Richmond Road
Putney, London SW15 2TG
Phone: +44 (0) 20 8785 5995
Fax: +44 (0) 20 8785 5985
www.murdochbooks.co.uk

Chief Executive: Juliet Rogers
Publishing Director: Kay Scarlett

Design concept: Heather Menzies
Design layout: Joanna Byrne and Wendy Inkster
Photographer: Jared Fowler
Stylist: Cherise Koch
Production: Alexandra Gonzalez

National Library of Australia Cataloguing-in-Publication Data
Title: Starters
ISBN: 9781741963472 (pbk)
Series: Kitchen Library: Notes: Includes index. Subjects: Starters
Dewey number: 641.812

Colour separation by Splitting Image
Printed by Imago in 2009. PRINTED IN MALAYSIA.

IMPORTANT: Those who might be at risk from the effects of salmonella poisoning (the elderly, pregnant women, young children and those suffering from immune deficiency diseases) should consult their doctor with any concerns about eating raw eggs.

OVEN GUIDE: You may find cooking times vary depending on the oven you are using. For fan-forced ovens, as a general rule, set the oven temperature to 20°C (35°F) lower than indicated in the recipe.